GW00832895

Day-by-Day Numerology

by Lia Robin

Do you know your lucky day? The best occupation for you? Who's waiting for you at the wedding altar? These are the questions everyone has, and numerology is the method that can give you all the answers.

Numerology is based on the belief that everyone has a special number. This number gives off a vibration, which ultimately leads to your individual destiny. *Day-by-Day Numerology* is not only a how-to guide on determining your number, but a guide book to your fate. It will provide the answers to the questions that are uppermost in your mind. You'll finally find out why certain life experiences keep repeating themselves, why you might have one ability and not another, and most important, how to make the decisions that will carry you successfully through your life.

Lia Robin was born in London. She moved to Paris, subsquently traveled to the East, where she studied myticism and became especially skilled in numerology. This is her second book on the subject. She lives in Paris with her husband and two children.

ASTROLOG COMPLETE GUIDES SERIES

The Complete Guide to Coffee Grounds and Tea Leaf Reading
Sara Zed

The Complete Guide to Palmistry
Batia Shorek

The Complete Guide to Tarot Reading
Hali Morag

Crystals - Types, Use and Meaning
Connie Islin

The Dictionary of Dreams
Eili Goldberg

Meditation: The Journey to Your Inner World
Eidan Or

Playing Cards: Predicting Your Future
Hali Morag

Day-by-Day Numerology
Lia Robin

Using Astrology To Choose Your Partner
Amanda Starr

Day-by-Day
Numerology

Lia Robin

Astrolog Publishing House

Astrolog Publishing House
P.O. Box 1123, Hod Hasharon 45111, Israel
Tel./Fax: 972-9-7412044
E-Mail: info@astrolog.co.il
Astrolog Web Site: www.astrolog.co.il

© Lia Robin 1998

ISBN 965-494-057-4

All rights reserved. No part of this publication may be reproduced,
stored in a retrieval system, or transmitted in any form or by any
means, electronic, mechanical, photocopying, recording or otherwise,
without the prior permission of the publisher.

Published by Astrolog Publishing House 1998

Distribution:
U.S.A. & CANADA by APG - Associated Publishers Group
U.K. & EUROPE by DEEP BOOKS
EAST ASIA by CKK Ltd.

Printed in Israel
10 9 8 7 6 5 4 3 2 1

Table of Contents

Introduction

Numerology is a mystical theory which claims that every number has a particular and unique vibration. These vibrations affect human beings or objects, just as sound waves or light waves do. The various influences lead to different results.

Numerology focuses mainly on the influence of the single-digit numbers 1, 2, 3, 4, 5, 6, 7, 8, 9, and at times on the numbers 11 and 22 as well. (In each chapter, there is a special note if the numbers 11 and 22 are also relevant to the analysis.)

Numerology assumes that each number has a basic "numerological number" that is obtained by adding up its digits. For example, we can take the number 76543 and add up its digits: 7+6+5+4+3 = 25.

As our aim is to reach a single digit, we add 2+5 and get 7. This result is what we use in the numerological analysis.

In order to calculate the numerological number, we reduce the basic data – date of birth, telephone number or house number – to one digit.

Numerology assumes that letters, as well as names, are connected to numbers. Each letter of the alphabet is linked to a specific number:

1	2	3	4	5	6	7	8	9
A	B	C	D	E	F	G	H	I
J	K	L	M	N	O	P	Q	R
S	T	U	V	W	X	Y	Z	

If we take a name, say **SARAH**, we write the numerical value next to each letter: S=1, A=1, R=9, A=1, H=8. We add up these five numbers: 1+1+9+1+8 = 20. We continue adding the numbers: 2+0, until we reach a single digit: 2. This is the numerological number for the first name **SARAH**.

Sarah's last name is **PETERS**; its numerological number is: 7+5+2+5+9+1 = 29 = 2+9 = 11 = 1+1 = 2

Note: Sometimes, the numerological number of the last name **PETERS** will be 2, and sometimes it will remain 11, according to the particular rule in each chapter.

Sarah's mother's first name is **RACHEL**, and its numerological number is 6.

Sarah Peters was born on 12.7.1955; the numerological number of her date of birth is:

1+2+7+1+9+5+5 = 30 = 3+0 = 3

The numerology in this book relates mainly to the individual's date of birth, first name, last name and mother's name. At the beginning of each chapter, the methods of calculation for that particular chapter are discussed in detail.

The Numerology of First and Last Names

The number corresponding to one's name is obtained by adding all the letters of the first and last names, resulting in one numerological number. The first and last names are written down, then the numerical values of the letters are added up and reduced to one digit, unless the sum of the numbers is 11 or 22. In that case, the number is not reduced to a single digit.

For example: JOHN SMITH

$$1+6+8+5+1+4+9+2+8 = 44 = 4+4 = 8$$

This is the number corresponding to John Smith's name. We then look at the number 8 and see what it means. You will see in the chapters that follow that it is possible to calculate a person's "spiritual qualities" (using vowels) as well as his "material qualities" (using consonants). Always check that both these sums add up to the name number.

(For JOHN SMITH, you will find that the vowel number is 6 [page 19] and the consonant number is 2 [page 30]. 6+2 = 8)

Name Number 1

You constantly aspire to express your personality in every original way possible. This is the epitome of your life's aspirations and objectives – to let your desires and ambitions run free, unfettered by the mores and constraints dictated by society.

You love privacy, and preserving it is given top priority in your life. If you really do desire to fulfill this ambition, you will be compelled to take responsibility for your life and not compromise. You will have to be sufficiently courageous to deal with the many obstacles in your path. Only by a difficult struggle will you reach your objective.

You enjoy being a pioneer in various fields and investigating new ideas. The pursuit of challenges and reaching the goals you have set for yourself in life cause the adrenaline to flow in your body. Every once in a while, you need to experience success as proof of your actions. It gives you satisfaction and encourages you to work toward the next objective.

Name Number 2

You are a person with a special sensitivity to others and to your surroundings. If you are to choose a vocation, social work, psychology or counseling would be good choices. There is no doubt that you would be very successful in these fields.

You are gifted with an extraordinary ability to listen to the needs of others, to be aware of their distress and sensitive to their desires. You are very patient and possess the sincere empathy and great love needed to understand others. Your intuitive abilities help you to comprehend other people's feelings and assist them.

You are overflowing with warmth and are able to give a lot of love to those around you. You always offer people warmth and sensitivity, as well as a shoulder to cry on. While you enjoy delicate and sensitive things, rudeness and coarse behavior offend you.

Name Number 3

You are essentially an actor. Gifted with theatrical talent, you love to perform in front of an audience and make them feel happy and uplifted. You enjoy making people laugh, thus providing them with an outlet for their tensions. Your talents manifest themselves in your verbal abilities and writing skills. If you combine your talents properly, you will benefit from all the facets of your personality.

Since you know how to entertain people and make them laugh, you could be a successful stand-up comedian. Every now and then, your ability to entertain and amuse enables you to extricate yourself gracefully from embarrassing situations.

Your ability to cause happiness, enjoyment and laughter is a source of much joy to you. You derive a lot of satisfaction from the fact that you are able to give of yourself to others. It may fill your life completely. Be careful not to spread your talents too thinly.

At times, you become too involved in your theatrical world. You may forget to be attentive enough to your family, focusing instead on your colleagues or other people. Avoid having too many fingers in too many pies, and do not let your attention stray from the most important things.

In spite of your acting talents and your ability to don masks without others being aware of it, you are honest and open by nature. You are able tell those close to you what you think of them – even if it is unpleasant.

Try to tone down your manner, since every now and then you are liable to offend someone unintentionally. Attempt to channel the talents you have been blessed with in positive directions that will be uplifting to others.

Name Number 4

You are organized and methodical. You know that only through hard, intensive work will you achieve maximum results. Work requiring precision and attention to detail suits you.

You are very disciplined, and when you set objectives for yourself, you achieve them at all costs. You are willing to forego other things as long as the fruits of your labor are perfect, at minimum cost and with maximum investment. You are gifted with a highly developed sense of responsibility and therefore others tend to trust you. You are honest and straightforward. These qualities help you in your professional life, but at times, within the jungle of modern society, you are perceived as naive.

Occasionally, you find yourself utilizing obsolete methods because of your fear of technology. You must be more open to new ideas. If you do so, you will be more efficient, and it will prove helpful both to yourself and to your surroundings. You are a perfectionist. You do not compromise on less than the best. You are bound by rigid conventions and expect others to be like you. You must be more aware of this tendency, since people are inclined to interpret such behavior as cruel and hard-hearted.

You tend to take things to heart. This might affect your health adversely, so you should make sure to take breaks from your fast-paced lifestyle – by taking a vacation, for example. It would be good if you had a regular program of physical fitness and watched your diet.

Always try to see the half-full rather than half-empty glass. This will teach you to enjoy the fruits of your efforts. You must be happy and smile more often.

Name Number 5

You are bubbly and love life – and quite unable to enjoy a quiet, tranquil lifestyle. You always need new stimuli and interesting challenges to keep you going.

You should try to be more patient and understanding. It is not easy for your partner to keep up with your frantic pace. Changes – which you are not only used to, but even require – may be threatening to your partner and may alienate him/her. Take life easier and more calmly.

You should choose a profession that involves working with people.

Make an effort to be calmer and more tranquil, less volatile and impulsive, and try not to become quickly addicted to various passions, as you are liable to do.

You must strive for a more balanced, full and whole life. This will make it easier for you to cope with your surroundings.

Name Number 6

You have the ability to give generously of yourself to those around you, without limitations. You are endowed with a highly developed sense of morality and justice, and social injustice enrage and revolt you.

You are able to put yourself in other people's shoes. The caring professions, such as social work or teaching, suit you. You are very generous and willing to share whatever you have with others, even if you have very little.

Your appearance is important to you. You are attracted to partners whose outstanding qualities are gentleness and fragility, and you avoid the company of vulgar people. You believe in working hard in order to achieve your objectives. You cannot stand receiving personal benefits or taking advantage of connections, and will always choose the longer but safer path over risky shortcuts.

Family is of utmost importance and you try to help out at home as much as possible. Your loved ones are so important to you that you sometimes clip their wings and do not allow them the freedom to do their own thing.

Do not rush to reveal your emotions in a new relationship. Occasionally, you are carried away by feelings and may end up disappointed. You must learn to navigate more independently through life and rely on yourself alone. Do not let others take advantage of your good-heartedness or your tendency to give of yourself limitlessly. Learn to give in moderation, otherwise you will find that others take advantage of you, possibly causing irreparable harm.

Name Number 7

Since you have been blessed with special spiritual qualities, you are able to help others as well as yourself. However, you will have to practice using this trait, as it does not manifest itself automatically. You possess sensitivities that others do not. You do not need other people to make you feel wholeness or enjoyment, as you are able to provide yourself with everything you need – interests, curiosity and a quest for knowledge.

Your natural spiritual qualities and unique abilities threaten to detach you from reality. Beware of overdoing your "visits" to these esoteric worlds. You must be firmly grounded in reality and everyday life in order to preserve your sanity and continue to function; you must also find a common language with the "mere mortals" around you, even if they do not share your spiritual gifts.

Do not become arrogant or indulge in delusions of omnipotence. Beware of setting yourself up as a miracle-worker. Remember that you are only a human being, and as such, your powers are limited. Be humble and act with generosity of spirit so that you may take full advantage of your qualities, both for your own benefit and for that of humanity.

Name Number 8

Your main strength lies in your ability to connect the material and the spiritual. Material success is very important to you and it is the yardstick according to which you measure yourself and your achievements. You are not afraid of hard work and are willing to make a great effort in order to attain your life goals.

Persistence is your key word and you do not give up easily, even if you do not succeed immediately. You appreciate efficiency, and when you begin a particular project, you work with great devotion. It is very difficult for you to withstand life's temptations. For this you need iron discipline. On the other hand, although the temptations are very attractive to you, you resist them admirably.

You have a tendency to exaggerate. When describing a situation either verbally or in your imagination, you tend to blow it out of proportion. This is a dangerous trait and may harm your credibility. It is crucial that you be aware of it and try to stick to reality as closely as possible.

You are impatient to reach a higher social status and become wealthy, but remember that the spiritual realm is just as important to you as the material world is.

For people such as yourself, the pursuit of wealth usually ends in disappointment. In the end, even if you achieve your goals and become wealthy, you will always feel that you have missed out on something.

You are never completely satisfied with what you have. If you feel guilty about the fact that your accomplishments at work are coming at the expense of your family, it is a sign that you should slow down. Be aware of your needs. This is the only way you will avoid malaise and a feeling of missed opportunities.

Name Number 9

This indicates the possibility of attaining wholeness. This wholeness manifests itself through the suppression of the desires of the moment, and by helping others, listening to their problems and being good to them. It is crucial that you learn to make others and their needs a top priority in your life, placing them before yourself.

You must learn to rise above petty concerns, and show nobility and generosity of spirit, even when in difficult and unpleasant situations. You are on a high spiritual level – one that demands commitment. Conserve your strength for the future, because you are not allowed to throw in the towel, even in the most difficult of times. The pleasure and satisfaction that you derive from life are not those enjoyed by most people. The better you treat others, reaching higher spiritual levels on your way, the more fulfillment you will feel by experiencing happiness and peace.

Name Number 11

You aspire to bring about peace in the world and the universe. In your eyes, all means are fair in realizing this lofty objective. You are even willing to endanger your life for these higher ideals as long as you know that you have done your best and given of yourself to make your vision a reality. You find it easy to get people to work toward realizing your dreams and visions. Society designates people with your intensity and power as leaders. Those around you know that you are able to work toward higher aspirations, and make sure that they are implemented.

Day by Day Numerology

You are pretty satisfied with yourself, with your abilities and with your natural talents. However, you must be cautious not to become pompous. Arrogant behavior will alienate people who might otherwise assist you in achieving your goals.

At the same time, beware of those who might exploit your power maliciously. Be alert! Keep your eyes and ears open for anything that might appear to stand in your way.

Name Number 22

You are superior to number 4, though basically you are made of the same stuff. You possess exceptional leadership abilities, and have been gifted with talents allowing you to excel as a leader.

You are very intelligent and have a highly developed manipulative ability. If you learn to take advantage of these characteristics in order to achieve the lofty goals in your path, there is nothing that you will not be able to accomplish. Beside leadership skills, you also have the makings of a politician or social activist: perseverance, efficiency, the ability to differentiate between the wheat and the chaff, clarity and sharpness of thought, and a phenomenal memory. You are able to recognize incipient social phenomena before others even notice them. You are gifted with acute analytical powers, as well as the ability to see things in their correct perspective and reach immediate decisions, which helps you attain your goals.

You must be aware of the needs of others as well as of social processes, so that you may define to yourself the goals and objectives that will result in social progress.

The Numerology of Vowels

In English, there are five vowels: A, E, I, O, U. These may be interpreted through numerology, and relate mainly to the realms of the spirit, the unconscious and the soul. The way to calculate them is very simple. Write down the first and last names, mark the vowels, and add up only the numerical equivalents of the vowels so as to obtain a single-digit number. If the result is 11 or 22, do not continue to reduce the number to a single digit.

For example: **JOHN SMITH**

Vowels: O,I

$$6+9 = 15 = 6$$

We will then look at what number 6 has to say about the person's spirituality.

Number 1

This indicates excellent abilities as a leader of the masses. You are ambitious and always aspire to succeed and race forward. This even permits you to push others around and elbow your way roughly.

You are original, innovative and uncompromising when it comes to quality. You are able to be independent and not take your talents for granted, but rather to hone them to excellence.

You tend not to listen to the advice of friends or others around you if you are uncertain of their intentions. While you are creative, you have an exaggerated degree of self-assurance. If you really wish to go far, you must keep the arrogant side of your nature in check and treat others with humility and respect.

The lack of patience that you occasionally display is liable to be a hindrance to you. You must learn to be more perceptive under certain circumstances, so as not to cause embarrassment to those around you. Being involved in public activities or politics would help you to develop the sensitivities and manners of a diplomat.

Number 2

You must be more assertive. You tend to agree with those around you and accept things even if you are not totally satisfied with them and would actually like to change them. You *can* do that; gifted with highly developed senses and awareness of what is going on around you, you are also able to discern subtleties. You are very tactful and have excellent diplomatic skills.

If it were up to you, the world would consist of nirvana alone.

It would not hurt if you developed a thicker skin to protect yourself from insults and offensive comments that are hard for you to take. If you found a way to cope with this kind of aggressiveness, you would no doubt be a happier person. You are very strong emotionally. People like you are the least likely to have a mental breakdown.

At times, you feel that you have the ability to lead the entire world. But this is not really so! Despite your spiritual abilities, your vulnerability does not permit it. It is preferable for you to follow other people's orders rather than aspire to leadership; in this way, you will be spared unnecessary suffering. You do not have the strength to stand up to the conflicts that this struggle involves.

You have the makings of a medium. The intensity of these traits may be frightening at times, but you must learn to use them for your own benefit and take maximum advantage of them.

Number 3

You are the kind of person who always gets along. Wherever you are, you invariably make friends and find yourself at the center of attention.

You are gifted with extraordinary acting abilities and excellent writing skills. You love company and will always be the life and soul of the party. You enjoy parties and social gatherings. Since you are always socially prominent and find yourself at the center of things, people invariably seek your company and want to be close to you. You know how to tell jokes and say the right thing at the right time. Other people never feel embarrassed in your presence, and you have the ability to make anyone – even someone you have just met – feel comfortable.

You are full of *joie de vivre* and cordiality. It is easy for those around you to be caught up in your cheerful mood. However, you are impulsive and must learn to control your desires and wishes of the moment. This is not always easy. If Number 3 is the sum of the vowels in your name, you must learn to concentrate on one thing rather than spreading yourself thinly over many areas.

Number 4

You have both feet firmly planted on the ground and are very realistic. You are able to see reality as it is without needing to embellish it. Anything that does not directly contribute to the cause is unimportant in your eyes. You are responsible and may be trusted implicitly.

You can be given authority without hesitation. You stick to the task at hand and strive to do it to the best of your ability. Your self-discipline is unwavering and you cannot be distracted until the task is completed. You are capable of doing work which demands a high degree of precision and perfection, work that others may shun due to its monotonous nature. While material things preoccupy you, you are not attracted to the spiritual realm.

You are able to converse about automobiles for hours, but an evening of poetry scares you off. Your schedule is so organized that it is difficult to make changes in your daily routine. You run your life meticulously and require order at home and in your head.

However, you are narrow-minded and not open to things and ideas that are new and different than those you already know.

If you were to broaden your horizons and allow yourself to open up to new worlds, you would find

Thank you for buying this book. If you would like to receive any further information about our product list, please return this card after filling in your areas of interest.

Title of this book..

If purchased : Retailer's name............................Town..

☐ Health and Nutrition
☐ Indigenous Cultures
☐ Occult & Divination
☐ Personal Growth

☐ Philosophy & Spirituality
☐ Psychology & Psychotherapy
☐ Women's Interest
☐ Other

Name...
Address...
....

AFFIX STAMP
HERE

DEEP BOOKS LTD
UNIT 13 CANNON WHARF BUSINESS CENTRE
35 EVELYN STREET
LONDON
SE8 5RT
UK

enjoyment in many things that you never even dreamed of doing or trying. Opening yourself up to new ideas and breaking away from rigidity would only be to your benefit.

Number 5

You are impulsive. It is difficult for you to control your momentary urges, and you often find that they take control of you and divert you from your original intentions.

You enjoy change to the point of obsession. If a week goes by without some special thrill, you will devise something to get excited about. You are not able to be calm for even a minute. You must always be in motion, and if you are not able to give vent to your impulses, you feel as if you are imprisoned. You like taking risks and walking on the fine line between a sane and orderly life and a crazy one full of experiences. Given your addictive personality, gambling, alcohol and so forth are tempting. You are advised to stick to the tasks at hand and control your dangerous urges.

You are sexy. Easily attracted to the opposite sex, you allow your fantasies to lead you down dubious paths which others would not even dare to imagine. You are obviously not one for routine work. If you were able to get away with not working at all and spend your days enjoying yourself, you would be in seventh heaven.

All this aside, you must develop a sense of responsibility and always be involved in the type of work that offers thrills and changes. If you choose a monotonous and routine job, you will not hold on to it for long. If you do indeed aspire to succeed in life and achieve high status at work or in business, you must learn to control your impulsive nature and focus on your objective.

Number 6

You are a classic family-oriented person. You prefer to neglect your career and anything else that may threaten your family and happiness – since for you happiness is linked to the amount of time spent with your family. You enjoy art and poetry.

The appearance of your home is very important to you, as you feel that it mirrors your inner self. The interior design influences your personality directly. You devote a great deal of attention to detail. You are blessed with a sense of responsibility and a desire to envelop those around you in infinite love. You must be aware of the fact that, at times, you are too generous with your love, and you should set some limits in this regard. Allow those around you, particularly family members, freedom. They are so important to you that your concern for their welfare is liable to drive you mad.

Calm down. Try to be less obsessive in your sense of responsibility towards your family. The more space you allow yourself and others, the more comfortable you will feel. You would also receive more positive feedback. Be open and broaden your horizons. Your natural characteristics and talents would manifest themselves to a greater extent if you focused on your abilities. Try to control your urge to constantly know what each member of your family is doing; you would waste less energy worrying. They will do just as well (if not better) without you pressuring them, whether consciously or subconsciously.

Number 7

Your character is that of a mystic. You pursue knowledge and seek a connection with your higher self – the soul. This trait may alienate you from others whose orientation is more earthy. Do not let yourself get carried away. Although this is very difficult, try to plant both feet on the ground. The more you succeed, the better your connection with your environment will be. People will understand you and you will find it easy to forge connections and make friends. The more you close yourself off in the bubble that transports you to mystical realms, the more difficult it will be for you to function socially. However, it is your choice alone.

You aspire to acquire knowledge and are not lenient with yourself in the process. When you want to achieve an objective, almost nothing stands in your way. You seek perfection in everyday situations as well as in more significant and serious endeavors. Beware of your natural tendency to be over-engrossed in spirituality. It might become an obstacle in your path to perfection.

Number 8

You are a forceful person with the ability to work hard in order to achieve your desires. Perfection and success in life are important goals for you. You do not always listen to the advice of others, even when you are sure of their good intentions. You have the traits of a lone wolf. You believe in yourself, and yourself alone, and find it difficult to cooperate with others. You have managerial abilities and could easily oversee a large staff or control extensive projects. For this reason, you should learn to include others in your decision-making and seek their assistance as a means of maximizing your success. Not only would you benefit from the help they can provide, but you would also be able to take advantage of their advice, guidance and experience. At times, you unintentionally hurt people's feelings. Be aware of this and learn to respect others.

You seek mental, physical and spiritual balance. This is the essence of your search in life, and those around you seem to think that you will not rest until you experience the pleasure of wholeness. To this end, you are prone to engage in extraordinary activity – a broad spectrum of activity, both mental and physical. You are able to begin your day very early in the morning, swim for an hour before work, rush off to work, attend a lecture on spiritual matters afterwards, and end your day by cleaning the house thoroughly. Usually, you reach a breaking point and find yourself falling on your nose, unable to function until you have renewed your energy. Learn to control your urge to experience everything, so that you will be able to reach the equilibrium you want.

Number 9

Your good-hearted and even over-generous nature may incite others to take advantage of you. While you need constant displays of love, at the same time you are not always able to give love in return. You have a highly developed artistic nature, and are an artist at heart. Since you are gifted with good hands, if you are not a painter or sculptor, you most certainly excel in another form of artistic expression, such as carpentry. You always know how to fix things at home and have an extraordinary ability to improvise. You are original, possessing a broad perspective that is unique and different. You invariably know how to take junk from the street and make something useful out of it, producing things which others would not even have dreamed of.

You strive to be knowledgeable and always try to read a lot. You are capable of reading an entire newspaper, including the gossip columns, just to be up-to-date on "what's happening". It is important for you to stick to reality. You do not allow yourself to float off to faraway worlds or simply to dream that your wishes will come true – just so that no one can ever accuse you of imagining unrealistic things.

Remember that you will always find yourself with both feet firmly planted in reality, because that is who you are. Therefore, you may occasionally allow yourself to let go and even delude yourself with dreams. If you do not dream, how will you fulfill your hidden desires?

Number 11

You have extra-sensory perception. You are able to sense things before they happen. You are intuitive and do not have to know someone for long in order to identify the dominant aspects of his personality. Spirituality is your strongest character trait. You have supernatural sensitivities, a subtle sense of discrimination and a need to lead others. You are extremely tactful. You can always be counted on to say the right thing at the right time and not cause others embarrassment. You are able to "sense" other people, to feel when those close to you are not well or if they are in distress, or, on the other hand, if they are happy and in a good mood.

Other may find that your special sensitivities can help them understand aspects of their personalities or know what steps to take in the future. If you learn to serve a broad public, both you and they will benefit. Your abilities may lead you to realms or achievements for which you have always yearned. Learn to make the most of your talents to foster justice and to have a positive influence, as these hidden powers might be misinterpreted by others; sometimes it is not possible to set these misunderstandings straight.

Number 22

You waver between lofty spirituality and practicality and purposefulness. You are ambitious, and as such, try to reach peaks that allow you to be active in several areas at once. You are aware that even the highest ideals can only be reached through a lot of hard work, and you are willing to shoulder the burden.

You have the ability to bridge the gap between people whose spiritual world is rich and full and those who belong to a more practical world and are characterized by earthiness and material things. You invariably find things in common with both sorts. Each of these aspects comprises a facet of your personality and contributes to your nature. You are never bored, whether surrounded by earthy people or by those whose interests lie in the spiritual realm alone. If you learned to take advantage of this unique quality, you and those around you would benefit greatly.

The Numerology of Consonants

The numerology of consonants relates to the material realm (as opposed that of the vowels, which concerns spirituality). The method of calculation is similar. Write down the first and last names, mark the consonants and add them up, finally reducing the results to a single digit. Again, if the result is 11 or 22, do not continue to reduce.

For example: **JOHN SMITH**

Consonants: J,H,N,S,M,T,H

$$1+8+5+1+4+2+8 = 29 = 11$$

We will then have a look at the interpretation for 11 to understand the material aspect of that person's nature.

Number 1

You are domineering. Although you are gifted with organizational and managerial skills and know how to get the most out of a team of workers, you occasionally achieve this in a rude and ruthless manner. Learn to use a more gentle approach. Sometimes, giving orders is not the best way to achieve an objective, as your subordinates will carry out your demands not out of desire or love, but because they have no choice.

Learn to channel your energy in positive directions. It will enable you to get the most out of yourself and out of the organization or staff that you head. Your managerial talents are noteworthy and your appearance inspires respect. You enjoy looking different than other people, although it seems as if you are afraid of this tendency. It is possible that over the years you have encountered cynicism, which has resulted in your fear. However, you must be open to the world and cultivate a stronger trust in others – it will enable you to give and receive more love.

Number 2

You are a very pleasant person. You are not aggressive and even if at times you express some aggressiveness, it is never vociferous and never takes the form of incomprehensible outbursts.

You exude pleasantness and amiability. People enjoy being in your presence.

You will never attack those around you nor will you take advantage of someone else's weakness. You are extremely tactful. Thanks to these qualities, it is very easy for you to make friends, and you are always surrounded by people. While preferring to stay in the background and not stand out, you definitely have a lot to say and have definite opinions.

You enjoy voicing these opinions and are aware of your intelligence. However, you will always find the right moment to speak your mind without being overly conspicuous and without causing provocation. See that you always preserve your uniqueness, as you usually succeed in doing.

You are not good at pretense. However, if you do not like someone, you will invariably hide your feelings and avoid him elegantly. On occasion, your sincerity lands you in embarrassing situations. However, if you stick to your own path – the one you usually follow, you may be sure it is the correct one.

Number 3

You are sociable and friendly, abounding with charm. People seek your company and especially want to be seen in your presence. You look great. Every color and fashion suits you. At any social event, you immediately become the center of attention. There is no doubt that you know how to take advantage of this situation, and make sure it brings small perks. You are particularly optimistic and view your life as lucky. You are quite hedonistic and enjoy the good life – fine dining, elegant night spots, and getting the most out of life. You love comfort and are definitely not one to go on long treks or sleep outside in a sleeping-bag.

Usually, you know exactly what suits you and how to plan your actions. Leaving things unresolved or unfinished bothers you, and it can be said that you aspire to perfection. At the same time, you do not demand the same degree of perfectionism from others, and this may be one of the secrets of your success and popularity amongst those around you.

From the negative point of view, you expect immediate gratification; if you do not get it, you act childishly.

Number 4

You have an neat appearance and enjoy organization and order. You are very pragmatic and meticulously adhere to an organized schedule. (It seems that in this case, a description which is brief and to the point is most suited to Number 4.)

Number 5

You are an interesting and unusual person, one who is considered unique and different by others. Gifted with a highly developed verbal skill, you keep your audience riveted with no difficulty. You are a multifaceted person, knowledgeable in a wide variety of fields. It appears that you are never bored. You will always find some interest in whatever you are doing, and invariably persist in your desire to investigate and delve into the deeper essence of things.

You abhor superficiality and shallow people. You radiate a love of life and adventure, enjoying special, unusual and different things. Occasionally, you are willing to take risks or act spontaneously for the fun of it or just to be unique and different. It is important for you to give free rein to your uniqueness. You love receiving compliments and have no problem complimenting others. You do not find it difficult to say something nice or put in a good word for a friend. You are honest, and hypocrisy is beyond you.

Although esthetics are important to you, first and foremost your friends must be smart and sensible; their external appearance is secondary in your eyes. However, you yourself always see to it that you look your best. At the same time, you deem it important to display your intellectual prowess.

Members of the opposite sex are attracted to you. You become bored quickly in a serious relationship and prefer changing partners frequently. Sex is central to your life, and it is rare that you find yourself without a partner for any length of time.

Number 6

You are a warm person who likes to shower others with love. You enjoy the warmth of the family unit. The members of your family constitute the most important element in your life – first and foremost, your children. You are generally crazy about children, and love your own to distraction. If your domestic life is successful, you will always be happy, since you believe that the pinnacle of happiness and success lies in a good family life.

Despite the fact that you are very devoted and faithful – at work too – you are the type of parent who will get home as early as possible in order to spend time with the children, bathe them and put them to bed.

You like helping others and have a highly developed sense of responsibility. When you are in the vicinity, your friends know there is someone on whom they can depend. Nevertheless, you have a strong character and are assertive to the extent that no one will dare make a sucker out of you or take advantage of your good nature.

You are very sober and view reality objectively. You

are not a wimp and know how to stand up for yourself and be tough when necessary. You also know how to cope with the difficulties of day-to-day living and face the rougher sides of life.

As you enjoy looking good, neat and rather elegant, you are fussy about your appearance. Physical activity is important and you make sure to set aside time for it during the week. You are gifted with a special sensitivity for *objets d'art*, and usually enjoy decorating your home with expensive and valuable pieces.

Number 7

You are shy and enjoy being alone. As an individualist, it is not always easy for you to communicate with others, particularly if they are strangers. You do not like sharing your experiences with others, even if they are very close to you.

You always look good, taking care to appear and dress well; you dislike looking unkempt.

You do not like being conspicuous and are always shy and retiring. Quiet by nature, you enjoy calm and tranquillity rather than public events or noisy parties. You invariably prefer quiet, peaceful recreation such as a movie or a meal in a fine restaurant to an evening at a nightclub.

You enjoy being involved in spiritual things and aspire to reach wholeness and nirvana. You tend to float in higher worlds; do not forget, however, that what keeps you afloat is equilibrium. You must therefore pay attention to the fine line between a healthy interest in the inner self and the soul – which provides you with equilibrium – and an extreme preoccupation with them that will upset it.

You must learn to be more down-to-earth. Strive to be more sober and not get carried away into spiritual realms that take you too far from those around you, causing you to lose the everyday connection with them. Take care not to get addicted to spiritualism and mysticism. There are people around you who love you, and those relationships are too important for you to lose them.

Number 8

Even if you have not yet achieved a position of financial status, there is no doubt that you are on the right path.

You are willing to invest many hours of work in order to attain the coveted success, which for you is mainly in the material realm.

You are gifted with excellent management skills and enjoy not only sounding important, but also looking so. You love expensive suits, sparkling jewelry, designer ties and matching cufflinks. Fancy clothes and nice things are *de rigueur* for you.

People tend to respect you even before they get to know you. Making an impression is very important to you; however, you also know how to be gentle, considerate and attentive to the needs of others.

If you are in charge of a staff of workers or if there are people who are subordinate to you, they never hesitate to come to you with their problems. They know that despite your impressive, high-power facade, you will be sympathetic.

You radiate charm and know how to captivate those who come into contact with you, whether at work or at play. Learn to give more prominence to your inner nature, as you have a lot to offer. Your inner aspects will help tone down your highly external side, and you will only benefit from such a move.

Number 9

You are gifted with the ability to adjust to any circumstances. You are in your element not only amongst dignitaries, intellectuals and the wealthy, but also amongst the simplest and poorest of folk. You get along with everyone. You do not make great demands on life, as you are easy to please and satisfied with what you have. You are resourceful and can make the best of even the worst conditions. You enjoy reading and are educated and knowledgeable.

A hopeless romantic, you enjoy writing poetry for your beloved and bringing her flowers. With regard to love and romance, you have no qualms about anything. Whatever you feel you must do to win your beloved's heart, you will do. Even if others view these actions as demeaning, you would never view them as such. You are blessed with a loving and warm heart, and enjoy giving of yourself.

Do not go too far, at the risk of becoming a nuisance or a burden to your loved one.

You have the qualities of an artist. If you get involved in the arts, you have a good chance of achieving impressive results.

Number 11

You have been gifted with rare qualities. As a result of your brilliant mind, you may undertake almost anything you choose and enjoy a high degree of success. An endless choice of possibilities awaits you. You can be involved in the humanities, become an academic lecturer or researcher, or, on the other hand, you might find your place in the sciences and become a doctor, mathematician, lawyer or scientist. You will definitely succeed in any field you choose.

On occasion, people find it difficult to understand what you are talking about, and you are forced to revert to simple words and ideas in order to be accepted as one of the gang. You have an unusual ability to lead people and sweep them off their feet. You could easily take advantage of this talent and get a huge crowd to accept your personal ideology.

Your influence over the general populace could be so strong and significant that it is worth your while to exploit your talents positively.

Number 22

Your goal is to reach the highest level. As you are on a lofty spiritual plane, you could make a substantial contribution to humanity. You must act responsibly, in light of your enormous abilities. You are capable of leading many people on any path that you choose, as others tend to believe you without hesitation. You must choose your path and actions carefully and wisely.

You are practical, efficient and very intuitive – along with extraordinary self-control and a finely honed sense of diplomacy. All of these qualities contribute to your image as a impressive person, one who easily captivates an audience. Others believe in you and your power. As your character exerts a strong almost magical influence over those around you, they are like putty in your hands. You must take care not to take advantage of this fact.

Initials – Balancing the First and Last Names

To obtain equilibrium between the last and first names of an individual, we must understand the number that results from the combination of the first letter of the first name and the first letter of the last name.

For example: **SARAH PETERS**

1+ 7 = 8

The number that balances the first name with the last name is 8 in this case.

Clearly, when one changes the last name (or the first name), the balancing number must be examined. Consequently, it is understandable why many people who change their name – their first or last name – retain the same initials.

Number 1

Follow your heart and listen to your inner voice. A lot of activity may bring you into equilibrium. Do not become static, since mobilizing energy and readiness for action will help fulfill your objectives. In addition, equilibrium may be achieved by avoiding dependence on others and sticking to your goal. The more you prove to yourself that you are able to reach your objective independently, the more chance you have of obtaining optimal equilibrium.

Number 2

Self-control. You will only reach equilibrium if you practice restraint and avoid impulsiveness. Think things through, plan ahead and do not give in to the impulse to act spontaneously. Even in unpleasant situations, do not make decisions until things have settled down. Do not take action when you are not thinking logically.

Number 3

Equilibrium is possible if you allow yourself to act on all planes. Do not curb your desire to express yourself artistically or technically. Find a way to express your hidden talents even if you are not sure that the result will be satisfying. Do not suppress your feelings – reveal your desire to love and be loved. Act spontaneously. You will find equilibrium if you are happy. You must allow yourself the possibility of expressing malaise and giving vent to your feelings. This will enable you to liberate yourself and reach inner places – places in which you may experience deep emotions and the joy of living.

Number 4

If you work hard, you will indeed achieve the desired equilibrium. Learn to exercise self-discipline and self-criticism and to enjoy the vocation of your choice. If you accept the results with love, you *will* reach equilibrium. It is important to achieve your objectives via the shortest route possible. Do not procrastinate; be productive. If you know how to reap the serious and significant fruits of your efforts, you will be able to enjoy them as well as achieve tranquillity and spiritual equilibrium.

Number 5

Equilibrium is obtained by action and movement. It is crucial not to become stagnant but to be constantly seeking, constantly in motion. Physical activity will relieve stress. Do not be fettered either by physical things that prevent you from being free, or by mental constraints that curtail freedom of thought. If you indulge in a great deal of action and movement, you will achieve equilibrium more easily.

Number 6

Involvement in the arts is an important step in your ability to achieve equilibrium. Learn to express yourself. You will reach equilibrium if you identify the sources from which you derive encouragement and support in times of need. It will also help if you take responsibility for your actions, even if they were not successful or turned out to be actually wrong. Your attraction to beauty and esthetics will ultimately lead you to the correct path toward achieving equilibrium.

Number 7

Remain in a state of mental tranquillity. The more you keep in touch with your soul and the higher world to which it is connected, the easier it will be for you to reach a state of equilibrium. Mental calmness, inner peace and involvement in the spiritual aspects of life will bring you equilibrium.

Number 8

You have the ability to channel your strength in positive directions. Doing so will bring equilibrium into your life. Do not allow yourself to be pulled in negative directions. Forcefulness is not necessarily a negative quality. Learn to take advantage of its positive aspects and to act in ways that will achieve equilibrium.

Number 9

If you do things for society and concentrate on your positive abilities to act on behalf of the environment and humanity, you will reach equilibrium. At the same time, you must set limits and not act in a manner that will negate your inner self. Do not get dragged into philanthropic endeavors that are out of the range of your human capabilities. If you act logically, you will obtain equilibrium.

The Date of Birth

The date of birth is the simple sum of the digits of the Gregorian birth date.

For example: 12.7.1955
$$1+2+7+1+9+5+5 = 30 = 3+0 = 3$$
The number of the birth date is 3.

If the sum is 11 or 22, do not reduce the numbers further. These are the numbers of the date of birth.

The date of birth is a very important guide to understanding an individual's long-term behavior, both in the past as well as in the future.

Number 1

The struggle to reach your goals and objectives never ends. As soon as you overcome one, another one immediately presents itself.

The type of decisions you make determines the results. The general direction is toward an expression of your inner self and your organizational and leadership abilities. It is important to depend on your unique talents and skills, and always to aim for the best, most successful results.

Number 2

Your desire is to live among a close-knit group of people. Your need to assimilate and mix with others allows you to cooperate well with them, and this will bring positive opportunities in the future.

Life teaches us to compromise. At times, it is necessary to let others take center stage and allow them to progress while you stand in the wings. Rely on those who are capable of giving you unbounded and unconditional love and support.

You have the natural ability to survive in difficult and uncomfortable conditions, and are extremely adaptable. You do not pursue status or esteem, and in general, although you do not seek prestige, you will obtain it as a result of your natural leadership qualities.

You have a tendency to be dragged into situations that encourage dependence and an inability to control your destiny and be your own boss. You are then deprived of the ability to think for yourself and act freely.

Number 3

You are offered many opportunities for working in different fields, particularly the arts. There are possibilities of achieving a level of spiritual wholeness and joy. The general direction points to freedom, the legitimization of different modes of expression, and release from narrow, limited thinking; there are also broadened horizons and openness resulting from the development of consciousness. You should avoid extreme actions, as they do not suit your personality. It is also advisable to exercise restraint and not to tempt fate. Taking the wrong turn may lead to uneasiness and consequently to a loss of self-confidence. It is worthwhile to be organized even if it is incompatible with your desire to be spontaneous and act according to your feelings. If something requires advance planning, making a list or a daily schedule, do it! Avoid unnecessary confusion that might impair your development. Structure, organization, order and planning will prevent you from landing up in difficult situations which will lead to undesirable results.

Number 4

Tremendous effort is necessary in order to attain the hoped-for results. Focus on the details and work thoroughly without compromising. Equip yourself with great spiritual strength and take a deep breath for the long haul ahead. Life demands that you practice self-control and restrain your impulses.

It is advisable to focus on the spiritual and the inner self, and not on external behavior and etiquette. Inner contemplation is necessary and is the right thing for you. At times, your emotional life ends up in failure and disappointment. Strong, stable mental foundations temper negative feelings. You are able to compromise and exercise moderation.

Extreme behavior will not lead to any development whatsoever, and therefore it is worthwhile to avoid rigidity and let your thoughts flow in various directions. Let your intuition lead you and make you attentive to what your heart has to say. Positive development will occur if you choose the path of compromise and openness to other opinions, new ideas and original ways of thinking. Avoid blaming others, especially when there is no solid evidence for doing so. People are never certain about the course that life may take, and are therefore in a constant state of apprehension and worry. You are able to carry a burden and suffer without complaining or revealing how difficult it is. Your ability to exercise restraint will stand you in good stead throughout your life.

Number 5

The direction of your life indicates surprises, changes and new experiences. You have the desire to examine, know and try out as much as possible. Your impulses drive you toward special and interesting fields. You will not rest until you have delved deeply into the essence of things – investigating, comparing and studying their secrets. It is important for you to learn and develop, and you often do this at the expense of other important undertakings. As the wise King Solomon said, "Life and death are in the hands of the tongue." Be alert to nuances and subtleties; emphasize that which must be expressed and downplay that which is destructive. If you choose to take advantage of the endless possibilities available to you, first take time to think and plan carefully, rather than acting on impulse. In your case, freedom of action parallels freedom of thought. Learn to control your desires and wishes, and try not to be swept away by emotion and urges of the moment. You have a strong desire to follow your momentary desires and obtain immediate gratification. Do not give in to them. Grappling with them may lead to clarity of mind and the possibility of controlling them. However, pay careful attention to these desires and be aware of their physical manifestations and what are saying. Relationships with members of the opposite sex are important and will help you get to know your inner self. Facing new situations and people of the opposite sex gives rise to feelings that are sometimes not expressed and creates opportunities to undergo new and interesting experiences. Do not reject these opportunities, even if they sometimes appear too risky at first.

Number 6

This indicates responsibility. Helping others is your top priority. Learn to control situations. Each action you take during your life should be taken in the spirit of love, and the desire to give and share. Your ability to empathize and identify with others is beneficial and serves your objectives. It presents endless possibilities to undertake a task and implement it. Your ability to face the future fearlessly gives you renewed strengths.

Given your excellent language and verbal skills, you are a good negotiator and a great orator. Your desire to help and be a good listener to those in trouble is a result of your ability to love. You are motivated by ambition and a desire to achieve. You never rest until the entire task is completed to the very last detail. You have broad vision and are able to cooperate with those around you. As a result of your sincere desire to cooperate and help, you succeed.

Number 7

Your perspective on life is unique. Look beyond the physical world to the path you must take. Spirituality constitutes an integral part of your life. You must aspire to a spiritual life as much as possible, and spend time on inner contemplation pertaining to the soul and God.

Strive to excel and specialize in a specific field. You must be very strong on the emotional level and know how to take criticism. It is important for you to be connected to your environment, feel the true rhythm of life around you and react as an integral part of society.

Number 8

There is fulfillment of your wishes, objectives, desires and aspirations. You have the power to make things happen. You establish yourself in positions of authority, high status and success, but you tend to ignore the fact that your relentless race to attain your objectives may disturb those around you. Try to avoid using power as much as possible, and assume positions of moderation wherever possible. Aggressiveness will get you nowhere. Avoid violent situations. Be assertive to the appropriate extent.

Money is all-important to you. You are willing to work hard and at various things, as well as do the impossible in order to accumulate as much money as possible. You view the possession of great wealth as a means of achieving all your objectives in life – from material things to the other aspects of life in which money plays a role, such as the ability to hold powerful positions of authority, control and respect.

However, there are also those who, although money is important to them, do not consider it their greatest achievement. If you are among these individuals, you find it more meaningful to be socially accepted as a person with high status, to be treated with respect, and to wield authority. Money is merely the means for achieving these goals, or the benefit that accompanies high rank.

Some number 8s consider money to be of equal importance to other things in life. If you hold this view, you will always find yourself somewhere in the middle – not highly influential, not with superior status, and not wealthy.

You are destined to face difficult situations which at times ionvolve quite a struggle. These situations are merely intended to help you develop, learn lessons and seek the equilibrium between the physical and the spiritual.

The amount of effort will determine the extent of success in life. Great efforts will bear fruit, and determination and perseverance will pay off in the end.

Absolute truth is the important thing in your life. If you follow the path illuminated by truth and do not deny it, you will learn to be sincere, both with yourself and your surroundings; you will certainly enjoy positive results.

Your skills are an excellent starting-point, and you

must learn to take advantage of them in the most positive manner possible.

The integration of material and spirit suits you. You must take advantage of the knowledge and experience you have accumulated throughout your life in order to utilize them correctly.

Number 9

This indicates bringing ideals to fruition. Your beliefs and ideals provide you with a broad perspective of life. You do not focus on details at the micro level, but rather see things at the macro level.

Your ability to differentiate between the wheat and the chaff enables you to have an overall view of life. You are not limited to or caught in standard molds.

You are able to develop creative and original thinking, and can consequently contribute greatly to human development.

Your power manifests itself in every aspect of your essence. It speaks of spiritual elevation, considered and responsible talk, and courage. There is danger in repressing these energies in the body, as they might erupt uncontrollably. It is crucial to utilize these energies and know how to control them.

Your potential ability is endless. You would be wise to focus on the needs of your immediate surroundings, then expand the circles gradually until you encompass the whole of humanity with your positive energies.

Number 11

You possess the qualities of number 2 – but magnified. This number is one of vision. The senses of responsibility and absolute control of life enjoy highest priority. Striving for success is important, but ideals are more so. You seek to help others, and all means are justified to attain this lofty objective. Primping, preening and pompousness are liable to work against you; uphold the principles of humility and inner integrity.

Your greatest preoccupation is with improving the world. You seek the best way of giving of yourself to your surroundings. You are able to bring positive energies and inspiration to those around you. However, you are enslaved by the constant need to receive positive feedback and a pat on the back. If you allow this need to control you, you will ultimately not be able to attain the lofty objectives whose fulfillment constitutes the essence of your life. Self-control is crucial along the entire path. The constant need to control life completely usually accompanies your path.

Number 22

Your measured, reasoned, responsible and even somewhat unhurried steps portend fine results. All your resources are directed toward one lofty objective, namely, helping others and showing concern for their well-being. At the same time, you are unable to remain firmly grounded in reality. This may be manifested in a tendency to sink into sweet, impossible illusion and the creation of a fantasy world. Getting rid of external influences and focusing on crucial aspects will allow strong, widespread action. You possess character traits that always enable you to stand at the apex of the pyramid. You determine the rules of the game: how to manage things and achieve joint objectives. Your uniqueness lies in your ability to do such things on a grand scale. You possess leadership qualities that can sweep large audiences off their feet, and your talents of oratory are highly developed. It is easy for you to influence people as if they were putty in your hands, causing them to follow you without hesitation. You are thorough and responsible and can exert unlimited influence over society, and from there, over the whole of humanity.

It's My Birthday...

The birthday number is a special number – it predicts and directs the events of the year between one birthday and another.

Let's say that someone celebrated his 22nd birthday. In other words, he was 21 years old and became 22 years old on a certain date.

Adding 21+22, we get $43 = 4+3 = 7$

Number 7 indicates what is in store for him during the coming year, between birthdays.

On his next birthday, he will go from age 22 to age 23.

$23+22 = 45 = 4+5 = 9$

Number 9 indicates what he may expect in the coming year, etc.

Usually, numbers 1 to 9 are considered. Some numerologists analyze number 11 as a separate number and do not reduce it.

Number 1

This may indicate that you are about to adopt a new position or take courses of action different than those you normally take. Keeping an open and flexible mind will help you immensely during this period of life. If you accept changes in life positively, it will help you adjust more easily to new situations. You must be aware of your state of health; it is possible that certain changes will affect your general health in the future. Be aware of the signals your body sends you and do not neglect them.

This is an excellent period for meeting new people, who will bring you genuine friendship. Listen carefully to your intuitive feelings and follow your heart. You can expect success at work. This is a good time, as there is the possibility of promotion or, on the other hand, of handsome profits. Family life may suffer. Invest more energy in domestic relationships and give more attention to those who are particularly dear to you.

Number 2

This indicates a change in location. Number 2 points to partnerships, either in your business or in your personal life, and may occur during times of economic difficulty or emotional blocks. You tend to be a good listener. During this period, you are not taking care of yourself as you usually do. You tend to invest a lot of effort in hard work, going into great detail. Focusing on peripheral things may prove destructive. It may also come at the expense of more significant things in life. Control your tendency to be a perfectionist. Unwittingly, you are neglecting other things that are significant to your future. This time of pressure will soon pass, so do not allow yourself to sink into depression or despair, even if your present situation appears bleak. You may depend on your partner. Get rid of some of the burden and responsibility you carry on your shoulders and you will discover that the resulting relief will influence your entire being.

Number 3

This indicates a desire to be at the center of things – to influence and lead – and it is possible that this desire will affect your distant future. This is a good time to establish relationships and acquire a high position in the company or institution with which you are affiliated. If you are not drawn to public activity, you may need to channel your energies elsewhere. Number 3 indicates artistic activity and the showing off of previously hidden skills. This is the time to publicize your work. Your self-confidence is stronger than it has ever been. You are able to withstand criticism. Do not hesitate to display your talents; it might pay off in the end and generate financial benefits.

This is a good period for professional development. Do not be tempted to stop studying in favor of something that may appear promising at the moment. Your studies will give you a significant boost in the future.

Number 4

You find it difficult to cope with change. Try to anticipate change and plan for it emotionally. There may be surprises in your family life, but they are less threatening.

This is a period of renewal. You have a strong desire to face your past mistakes and turn over a new leaf. Take advantage of the openness which characterizes this period of life to learn the lessons of the past. Be brave enough to implement them.

By nature, you enjoy routine. Therefore, it is advisable that you do everything in your power to weather these temporary disturbances quietly and return to a routine that brings you peace of mind and plenty of self-confidence. Pay careful attention to family-related problems, and mobilize all your efforts in order to solve them in the easiest way possible, without causing unnecessary commotion.

Number 5

The focus here is on business. This period provides opportunities for becoming financially established. You focus and concentrate on what you do, without giving in or compromising when it comes to quality. The actions you take during this period will serve as milestones for your future, both in life in general and in business in particular.

You are open to meeting new people and your communication with your surroundings will blossom in the near future. The long-term effects will be revealed through your growing trust of others.

During this time of life, your managerial abilities may emerge. Even if you never thought yourself capable of such work, this is a good chance to move into positions of management and supervision. Those hidden aspirations might now be realized. Be courageous and implement your ideas.

Number 6

This is a good time to take a break from work and do things around the house. If your home is in need of renovations or repairs, this is the right time to do them. It is not a good time for travel or for leaving the home and family. This is the time, more than ever, that it is vital to listen to family members, offer them help when needed and stay close by!

It is also an excellent time to bring the family together; you should take advantage of it, as it will influence later periods of life and help ensure open and honest relationships with family members. Decisions should be made after due consideration and planning. All possible risks should be recognized and taken into account.

During this period, you may experience confusion and dissatisfaction, and it is therefore advisable to act thoughtfully and responsibly, *not* allowing things to take their own course.

Number 7

Your spiritual nature will come to the fore and therefore you should be open to change and allow energies to flow freely. Your inner power is growing, and with it, your capacity to cope in times of crisis. You will emerge stronger from this period. Your self-confidence will increase and you will be more aware of the emotional processes taking place in your life.

Be aware of any physical change or any problem. The more you are aware of your body, the easier it will be to overcome health problems and catch them at an early stage. Do not neglect your health. Your body is exposed to crises at the moment, which may affect your constitution. Prepare yourself for this.

Money that you have been expecting will be delayed. Proper money management is crucial at this time. Do not make mistakes and assess your business correctly. Only in this way will you ensure your economic status and security.

Number 8

This is the time to achieve the goals and objectives that you have aspired to for a long time. It is an excellent time to realize your aspirations and implement grandiose plans. Do not miss this opportunity; take full advantage of it! Your material situation will be good during this period, and you will be successful in business or at work. Expect a promotion or unusually positive feedback from your superiors.

At the moment, the timing of whatever you do is crucial. It will affect the course of things.

Do not let peripheral issues distract you. Act without undue hesitation so that you do not miss this golden opportunity.

Avoid extravagance, and be careful how you spend money. Your desired objectives may require the investment of a hefty sum of money. Consider carefully if it is actually worth your while, and plan your steps judiciously.

Number 9

This is a time of completing circles, bringing things to a close. During this period, tasks that you have undertaken will reach a successful conclusion. You are completing a cycle and ending another chapter in your life; however at the same time, you are beginning a new cycle and a new chapter. This process of closure energizes you for a new beginning.

There may be separations from people you love, and renewed connections with others or you might make new friends.

In addition, there may be crises – either material or spiritual. In any case, you will emerge strengthened, which will help you to cope with different kinds of crises during the next stages in your life.

Number 11

This period of time is characterized by an ability to be less critical towards those around you, and to accept things as they are. There is less fighting and arguing, and more understanding, empathy, sharing and wishing to help others.

The harmony that will reign is only temporary, so you should take advantage of every moment to derive the maximum benefit for yourself.

Inspiration enables you to calm down. You can take advantage of qualities flowing out of your inner energies.

The inner peace and tranquillity that you are enjoying at the moment help you to understand processes to which you were oblivious until now. You are open to new and exciting discoveries that affect other stages of your life.

The Nine-Year Cycle

The nine-year cycle is actually a cyclical prediction for the next nine years. The difficulty always lies in determining the first year of the cycle. Once determined, we know what will occur in the years that follow.

The year is determined as described below:

Date of birth (the month and day) – reduced to a single digit, plus the year during which the inquiry is being made – reduced to a single digit, minus the thousand and hundred digits – not reduced, plus the individual's age – not reduced.

For example:

Date of birth: $12.31 = 1+2+3+1 = 7$

Year of inquiry: $1996 = 1+9+9+6 = 25 = 2+5 = 7$

Minus the thousand and hundred digits: -19

Age: 26

Total: $7+7+(-19)+26 = 21 = 2+1 = 3$

Therefore, for the date of birth given above, 1996 will receive the number 3; 1997 – number 4; 1998 – number 5; 1999 – number 6; 2000 – number 7; 2001 – number 8; 2002 – number 9; 2003 – number 1; 2004 – number 2; 2005 – number 3.

This final number begins a new cycle of 9 years.

Note: If the total is a "minus" number, we relate to the number only and ignore the minus value.

For example:
Date of birth: 1.1
Year of inquiry: 1996
Minus the thousand and hundred digits: -19
Age: 5
Total: 2+7+(-19)+5 = -5 = 5

Number 1

A good year! This is the time to broaden your knowledge in areas you always wanted to explore but never did. You now prefer to sever ties with people who limit you or hold you back. You are more than ever willing to try new things and you are open to new ideas. Take advantage of your developing sense of boldness and desire for innovation.

If until now earthly things distracted you and prevented you from engaging in inner contemplation, this is the time to devote time to yourself. Re-familiarize yourself with different aspects of your personality and get to know the ins and outs of your soul and your inner world which has been neglected until now.

Number 2

By the end of the year, you hope to reach a much higher point than where you started at the beginning of the year. It is important to you not to get stuck in a rut. You do not settle for simply maintaining the status quo. This strong, relentless desire to reach higher levels and greater achievements in life will accompany you throughout the year. You are liable to experience great disappointment if in the final reckoning you feel that you did not succeed in attaining the objectives you set for yourself at the beginning of the year.

Number 3

This is a positive year that will bring you great happiness. However, you must seek it. If you sit back and wait, there is no certainty that you will reap all the benefits that this year may bring. You may experience things that you did not even dream of experiencing. Achievements will follow the hard work and efforts of previous years. You will finally reap the fruits of your labor, and the rewards will be greater than you ever imagined. You will always be in the right place at the right time, and have your cake and eat it too! The timing of surprises will always be in your favor. Take full advantage of this situation.

Do not hesitate to express yourself and your ideas. Muster your self-confidence. Your ideas will be granted renewed validity, and your friends will hold you in higher esteem than ever.

Your inner freedom and sense of release are intoxicating. Do not be tempted to be swept away by these feelings. Restrain yourself and set limits so that you will not find yourself leaping from one extreme to the next. Go with the flow and let yourself be led to new discoveries of yourself and of others.

This year is one of new beginnings in various areas affecting your future. Far-reaching changes may come your way this year, perhaps even unexpectedly, without prior warning.

For public servants, this will be a year of public recognition. Finally, after years of effort and hard work, you will reap the fruits of your labor. Success will be far-reaching, and surprisingly so. The more careful you are with the social side of things, the greater your success will be.

Even during difficult times, you must maintain high morale and good spirits. It will help you overcome crises and influence your immediate surroundings. The more restraint you display, not allowing your spirits to fall, the more those around you will hold you in high esteem.

Number 4

A year of financial progress. The reason for this might be a promotion at work or the start of a new business. You must be practical and responsible. Plan your steps in advance; be thoughtful and decisive. You should not leave things to fate, nor be hasty. It is advisable not to work too hard; do not overdo things.

You should not act based on your discretion alone, even if your intuition is usually correct. In this case, it is preferable not to act spontaneously or rely on your senses, but to rely on cold logic alone. Do not let external diversions distract you from your goals. You have to show determination in order to succeed. Try to eliminate distractions and concentrate on the task at hand.

Try to be more assertive as this a year offers opportunities for progress and success. Consequently, those who come in contact with you will respect you and hold you in high esteem.

Do not underestimate yourself. You radiate self-confidence. The more you develop your sense of self-respect and believe in your abilities and endeavors, the better those in your environment will relate to you. Control yourself and do not let yourself get dragged under by the ceaseless undertow of ambition. Devote time to your home and family.

Number 5

This is a year which brings variety to your life, and you should be rational and calm as it goes by. It is a year in which you will learn to recognize the differences between people.

You will learn to appreciate opinions and ideas that oppose your own, and to hear them out with patience and understanding. During this year, you will find out whether you are a sociable person or not – one who is easily assimilated into society, likes other people and is open, or one who is more reserved and tends not to form immediate ties with others.

It is a good year to become involved in things that seemed a waste of time in previous years. During this period, you will learn to appreciate the importance of taking up leisure activities and to value the new content that they bring to your life, as well as the unique character and energies that they provide in an otherwise routine existence. A new relationship will infuse your life with "new blood" and make you feel young again.

Number 6

This year provides elements of stability regarding all the basic components of life: home, family, work and friends. This is a year during which you can make changes and decisions that will turn out for the best.

It is an excellent year for developing creativity. Get involved in the various aspects of the arts, handiwork and crafts.

The year will provide a good and positive atmosphere for study, and will inspire confidence, self-discipline and self-control. Involvement in the arts and spiritual things could become so significant that the general course of your life may change.

It is crucial not to dominate those around you, not to discriminate against others, not to brand people with stigmas and not to employ a double standard.

And finally, this is a year in which you will learn to appreciate pure, honest love, without the need to receive anything in exchange or "settle accounts" with the other side.

Number 7

This is a good year for the spirit – a year of spirituality. However, do not flee from reality; make sure you have both feet firmly planted on the ground.

Concentrate on the present and on the future. Dwelling on past mistakes will not be helpful to your progress; on the contrary, it will cause you to remain in the same place. Instead of concentrating on the past, try new modes of action and move forward.

The more you introspect, the easier it will be for you to examine your inherent abilities. During this year, you will be able to arrive at your inner truth. It is a good time for soul-searching.

You are standing at a crossroads in life, trying to decide which path to follow in the coming years. Giving to others and doing things for their welfare may contribute significantly to the feeling of wholeness you yearn for.

Number 8

This year should have good results: joint investments, successful joint business ventures, or the possibility of receiving a large loan from a friend, which will lead you to handsome, unprecedented profits.

Give backing and support to those around you who require it. Be sensitive and listen carefully to the needs of the people close to you. Try to assist them in any way possible. You too will benefit, as *you* will also be able to lean on *them* in times of need and receive their support.

Give of yourself in a broader forum as well. You will become aware of the contribution you have made to others and it will create in you a sense of satisfaction and a feeling that you are doing the right thing.

Number 9

This is the right year to finish things you began in the past. It is very possible that the efforts you are making at work, business or in the home at the moment will only bear fruit in a number of years. However, you will certainly see results.

There Is An Answer To Every Question!

Here is a simple method to answer questions by means of numerology:

Think of the question or issue; choose three numbers randomly; for example, open three books and jot down the page number, or choose three telephone numbers, or just think of three different numbers.

Next, add the numbers up; the number you reach will direct you to the answer. If the sum is 11 or 22, do not continue to reduce the number to one digit.

Number 1

This indicates new work (in the karmic sense, in other words, something that must be done). This is a good time to exchange the old for the new; also, anything regarding changes or renovations at home. A good time to take the initiative and responsibility. Control over actions and demands is necessary now. Try to move forward and progress with time.

Number 2

This contains elements of strong feelings which are manifested in the ability to understand other people's situations, share their experiences from the emotional point of view, and empathize with them. Number 2 symbolizes the ability to discern subtleties. There is good intuition. This is not a time to be closed or isolated. Be more sociable and less of an individualist. This is not the right time to make decisions. Leave them for a later date.

Number 3

Be thrifty and weigh your actions wisely. Do not act hastily, as this might cause you to make mistakes. It is important to plan and act responsibly. This number symbolizes release from crises. Act in a logical and thoughtful way. Do not let emotions control your more rational, cold and logical side.

Number 4

This indicates efficiency, practicality, the desire to focus on the main task at hand and discard the insignificant. There is a demand for harder work and greater effort, and you must not leave things undone. Be consistent and very diligent. This is not a good time for a vacation or idleness. Take advantage of every spare moment to finish projects and attain objectives that you are close to.

Number 5

There is sexual and interpersonal tension. Number 5 symbolizes relationships in which the dominating factor is sex. Sensuality is most important, as well as the ability to communicate. Number 5 represents communication, new places and new possibilities, along with a failure to control impulsive reactions. There is a desire to try everything, and an inability to stay in one place for long.

Number 6

This indicates an attempt to innovate in many fields. There is a desire to change old habits or get rid of old things. There is an urge to give to others and project the energies which are bottled up in the body and soul outward, in order to promote goodness and love in the world.

Number 7

There is a desire to see the world through rose-colored glasses, along with a blatant disregard for the rougher aspects of life, for frustration and anxiety. Be realistic and objective to the best of your ability. Beware of being led astray. Restrain unconditional trust and be emotionally willing to correct wrongs and injustice.

Number 8

This symbolizes a good financial situation and high economic status. The goals you have set for yourself are now closer at hand than ever before. Your financial abilities have increased and will now be realized. Without a strong will, you cannot achieve your goals and objectives. Stick with your desire and neutralize anything that gets in your way – either by material means or by means of strong emotional and spiritual forces.

Number 9

Any endeavor you have undertaken will now be completed in the best way possible. Do not start new projects right away. This is a good time to make long-range plans. Learn from past mistakes and plan your next steps accordingly.

Number 11

This is an excellent time to devote time to the home and family. Do not put aside things that you have begun – finish them. Take advantage of your teaching and instructing skills in order to assist family members or close friends. They are likely to benefit greatly. Avoid getting involved in far-fetched ideas, and do not attempt to force your opinions or ideas on others – particularly on members of your family.

Number 22

Exploit this time and plan it well so that you will have the opportunity to realize your aspirations and plans to the maximum. Do not be tempted by power or money. Be sure that you are doing your best without thinking of the benefits that might result from your actions.

Giving Answers According to the Clock

This is a wonderfully simple and efficient method to respond to a question or issue by means of numerology.

As soon as a question is asked, look at the clock and note the time. It is important to consider the hour as part of a 24-hour day. Supposing the time is 3:20 p.m., and it is Wednesday.

Hour: 15
Minutes: 20
Day of the week: 3

Add up all the numbers and you will get 38. Reduce it to one digit and the result is 2. We will then read about number 2 and address the question or issue with the interpretation as our guide.

Number 1

You are characterized by independence and the need to be a leader. This number indicates a person who does not suffer from burnout, has good spatial orientation, and does not compromise. Your mental ability overrides your emotional capacity. You desire greatness, importance and fame.

Number 2

This shows a desire to give and receive in small quantities, as well as an inability to make weighty decisions on your own, and a yearning for peace, brotherhood and love. You have a lot of patience and tolerance for those around you.

Number 3

This indicates building and creating new and original things. You are unable to stand by and watch the distress of others, and desire to help all living beings. You abundant cheerfulness and amiability pervade the environment. Your tremendous sensuality is expressed through love of the physical, the sensual and the sexual.

Number 4

This indicates planning and organization, discipline and responsibility. You have the ability to undertake long-term projects and shoulder complex emotional tasks. You have a strong desire to influence your surroundings, and an unconditional love for family members.

Number 5

This shows an impulsive nature and an inability to tolerate a routine or a monotonous life. You want to live life to its fullest and make the most of it. You love the good life, hedonism and the gratification of impulses and immediate needs.

Number 6

You have the ability to discern subtleties and benefit from different situations or opportunities. You know how to manifest your inner tranquillity and self-discipline. You give of yourself to others and care about them. You do not consider economic status important and you do not pursue wealth.

Number 7

Inner contemplation – getting to know your inner self and being – is important to you. You feel the need to express your unique talents and to achieve peace of mind. This is a good time to take a break from the rat race or to study.

Number 8

Pay attention to detail and analyze problems in order to find their solution; do not mislead others or take short-cuts on the path to your objectives. You want to stand up for your principles without compromise. It is important to experience new ways and adopt new ideas.

Number 9

The wish to give without limits goes beyond the boundaries of logical thinking. Your emotions are very strong and your decision-making ability is weak. You have a desire to be creative and to bring your inner feelings and hidden talents to the fore.

Daily Prediction

It is possible to try and predict the nature of a particular day. In order to do so, we utilize a simple method. Take the first name number of the person, add the number of the day of the week (1 to 7) and the number of the week in the month (1 to 5).

For example:
Sarah: The first name number is 2.
Tuesday: The number is 2.
The third week in the month: The number is 3.
2+2+3 = 7

We can make a prediction for that particular day by reading about number 7 in the descriptions that follow.

Number 1

At the end of this day, you will feel that it has been productive and not just another day. Matters that you had been putting off and that you were worried would not get done, should be dealt with today. The chance of getting a positive result is better than ever. People will be more attentive and amenable to you, and you are advised to be efficient and practical in order to take advantage of this day in the best way possible.

It is a day charged with positive energies which will help your longed-for dreams or plans come true. You must be consistent and rather ambitious in order to achieve your objectives. Do not be intimidated, even if it seems that you are unable to face the demands your objectives make of you.

Number 2

This is a good day for thinking about details. You might find yourself involved in grandiose plans which, in the end, will not be feasible. This day may begin on a positive note and end on a negative one. You might be in a good mood at the start, and become depressed towards the end. Therefore, you should be very cautious in your thinking and decision-making. It is preferable to consult with experts on different matters than to take the initiative and responsibility for things you know little about, and then suffer the consequences.

Today, focus on planning rather than on implementation. It is a good day to be at home rather than going out and engaging in all kinds of activities. The benefits of staying at home will be ten times greater than those you might derive from going out.

Number 3

This is a good day to concentrate on one type of activity. If you spread yourself too thin, it could limit your capacity to reap the greatest benefits from this day. It is not a good time to get involved in economic or financial matters. This is the right day to be frivolous; do not think too much or behave too seriously. This is a day of *joie de vivre* and expressions of joy. Do not let other things bother you today. Take advantage of this light-heartedness to recharge your energies.

Number 4

Do not try to surprise others today, or attempt new things. On the contrary: Act as you usually do. A new experience or unplanned action is liable to end in failure.

Today, it is preferable to be sure of each step and consider your actions wisely and carefully.

Number 5

This is a good day for meeting new people and mixing with others. If you have a fear of crowds or of meeting new people, this day will help you overcome these fears and you can take advantage of this time to make social headway.

Number 6

Today, it will be worthwhile to get out of the house and celebrate or commemorate an important event in the presence of other people. Go out and enjoy yourself at a club, restaurant, café or disco. Just see that it matches your mood and suits the people who are with you. Joint undertakings will be successful.

Number 7

On a day like today, you must let your body be calm and allow your soul to wander off in various directions. Rest and tranquil thoughts are good. It is worthwhile to do a bit of soul-searching and begin to make long-range plans.

Number 8

This is a good day to implement important projects that involve a lot of work over a long period of time.

Today, it is preferable to concentrate on *doing* things. Whatever you do today will have favorable results and serve as a basis for future success. Do not waste energy on differences of opinion or futile arguments. Act decisively, according to your plans, and do not stray from them.

Number 9

Today, it is crucial that you take advantage of your personal abilities and special skills. You should devote some thought to your professional future or to new ways of making a living.

If you act on behalf of others today, you will be greatly appreciated for your time and effort.

Seeing Others Through Numbers

Are you interested in knowing the nature or dominant qualities of another person, even a total stranger? No problem! Simply look at him or her and think of a number from 1 to 9. As soon as you have "picked up" on the number, check its interpretation according to the following descriptions. (It does not have to be the individual's personal number.)

Number 1

These people inspire in their spouses a sense of security and a feeling that they are in good hands. They are productive and very bright, sharp-tongued and decisive.

Number 2

These people do not always know how to stand up for their rights, but are willing to share what is theirs with others and give of themselves endlessly. They do not like chaotic or noisy places, and prefer spending their leisure time in a quiet romantic setting rather than in a busy place packed with people. On occasion, they can be a bit closed, but if they are encouraged to speak, they will be very sociable. They like volunteering and contributing to and improving the quality of life in the place where they live.

Number 3

These people always look happy, and even during times of crisis or pressure, they will always be cheerful. They always remember birthdays and eagerly await any celebration or event. They are usually organizers, whether of projects or of events. They have extraordinary analytical skills which they apply so as to get the most out of the various situations they find themselves in during their lives.

Number 4

These people cannot stand hypocrisy or lies and are liable to sever relationships with others if they suspect a lack of honesty. They enjoy being alone and are never bored on their own. They always like what they are involved in.

They are avid readers who can even be described as chronic book worms. They will read anything: books, newspapers, magazines, etc. They are interested in many fields and, being very knowledgeable, may be described as "Renaissance people". They take an interest in everything – from politics and current events to sports, theater, dance, music and art.

Number 5

These people enjoy adventure and traveling to special, unconventional destinations. They are unpredictable and may surprise others by breaking their routine in amusing ways. They radiate joy and people love to be near them because they are never boring. Their minds are never at rest and they are always busy planning something, finding new and original ideas. Not only won't they settle for less – they always want as much as possible!

Number 6

These people appreciate expensive items and enjoy a life of luxury. They like quality goods and will not buy inexpensive, short-lived things; they would rather buy the most expensive items that will last for years. They like bright people with academic degrees, as well as researchers and scholars. They are not able to make friends with those whom they consider their inferiors. Their arrogance does not bother them at all and they are indifferent to what others think of them. Neither malicious gossip nor spiteful talk upsets them.

Number 7

These are slow people. They like taking their time and getting through their day at their own rhythm. They find it difficult to break their habits, and they like their immediate surroundings, the warmth of the home and their own little corner. They enjoy a good movie or meal and anything that adds spice to life. They do not like noise and prefer to live in a calm and quiet environment. They prefer country life to city life. They love their children very much, but they find it difficult to tolerate the noise made by other children or to take care of other children. Spirituality rules their lives and at times they lose their sense of reality and time.

Number 8

These people are calculating and consider each step carefully. They always consult professional experts before taking action and never accept just one opinion; they rely upon two or more opinions for business transactions or major decisions. They are workaholics and their work is just as important to them as their families. They are responsible, serious and rational. It is difficult for them to be spontaneous and act without a plan, even when it comes to things that are not connected to their work. Their daily schedule is always carefully planned and full. They invariably know what they will be doing in the next few months. If some aspect of their plans does not materialize, it is liable to shake them up and undermine their self-confidence.

Number 9

These are people with strong and solid principles who like helping others, particularly the weaker social strata. Social justice is important to them and they abhor social iniquities. It is important to them to persuade as many as possible people to adopt their ideologies. Economic concerns are not central to their lives, but they try to establish a firm economic basis and create a financial status for themselves so that they might have the means for disseminating their ideas and ideologies.

The Partnership Number

When two people are married or committed to each other, their partnership number can tell us about their future.

This number is obtained by combining their personal numbers. Remember: The personal number is calculated from their first and last names prior to any change which may have taken place as a result of marriage.

For example:

SARAH PETERS

1+1+9+1+8+7+5+2+5+9+1 = 49 = 13 = 4

JOHN SMITH

1+6+8+5+1+4+9+2+8 = 44 = 8

The partnership number is 4+8 = 12 = 3.

Number 1

The partners must be clear about each other's limits, and learn not to impinge on the other's territory or personal space. Each one must respect the other's wish for privacy. They have very different personalities and areas of interest; this means that they are two individualists who, if they are squeezed together, might go their separate ways for good. If each one learns to respect the other's desire for true freedom, there is a greater chance that this partnership will last. Each must exercise a certain degree of self-control and practice restraint – even when this is very difficult or when he/she feels deprived of their partner's attention.

Number 2

Both partners must work hard at cooperating. Without this cooperation, the partnership will not survive. They must be patient and understanding with each other during times of crisis, and must learn to live in harmony. Momentary outbursts must not be allowed to cause rifts in the relationship. They must beware of getting involved in a power struggle. The more they cooperate with and listen to each other, the more successful their life together will be.

Number 3

Difficulties in communication may undermine even a relationship based on love. The partners must learn to express themselves, whether for solving problems and releasing pressure verbally, or for sharing their feelings of love and affection verbally – not only physically.

Good and open communication is a vital basis for the relationship. The partners must learn to share their experiences and tell each other what is going on in their hearts and souls. It is important to know how to express joy and not be repressed or restrained. The better they are at sharing and expressing joyful experiences, the more complete and rewarding their lives will be.

Number 4

The partners must reach completeness in their life together. They must learn to implement ideas, initiate and organize. This is the catalyst for their life together. The better they are at working together toward joint objectives, the stronger their ties will be. Idleness and inertia may dull their life.

Even if they are not blessed with a high energy level, it is worthwhile to be busy: producing, planning, organizing, initiating, being in action. Creative thinking produces new ideas. If the partners are idle, they will very soon experience boredom and tedium which will undermine their relationship.

Number 5

This number indicates the need to learn to accept the concept of a process, of things changing. An unrestrained life together – in which the partners are unable to maintain a balance, to plan ahead or to be rational, but rather usually behave as if they have been swept along by their feelings or actions – is liable to end badly.

The more the partners control their passions and immediate needs as well as delay gratification, the more planned and organized their life will be. This is likely to bring order into their lives, and this order will give them a sense of greater self-confidence, leading to the right way of life.

Number 6

The partners must learn to take responsibility and not blame each other every time something happens. Developing creativity is crucial for living together. Giving free rein to positive energies and using creativity to express what is deep in the soul is most welcome. The partners must learn to love!

The ability to open their hearts to love generally and unconditionally will provide the partners with a new perspective on their relationship.

Number 7

The partners must work together spiritually and develop their intuitive abilities. Sensitivity – going into detail and developing the rare skill of discerning subtleties – is likely to improve interpersonal relations substantially. If both partners "broadcast" emotions and thoughts and "sense" each other, they can expect to live together in harmony.

Number 8

The partners must find the balance between them. Usually, they are pulled in different directions. They must try to maintain a relationship in which they are able to find a common ground. Money is valuable and important in life, but no more important than the need to give expression to the soul. The couple must not let their lives become a continuous quest for material things, nor should they become acquisitive; having said this, they should not turn their lives into a constant search for spiritual fulfillment.

Number 9

The partners must be open to others. They must learn to love other people rather than just themselves. Giving to others and the desire to give of themselves as much as possible is likely to lead them to the realization of the immense inner powers with which they have been blessed, and to elevate their relationship to a higher spiritual plane.

One and Another and Another and Another...

Every connection which links more than one person, from marriage to a soccer team, can be examined easily.

The personal numbers of the various participants are collected (the partners or team members, for example) and added together until a single digit is obtained.

This is their "relationship" number. (In the list, the examples are general ones. Wherever the word "couple" appears, you can substitute "team" or "partners", and vice versa.)

Use this method for combinations of three people or more, and use the partnership number (page 84) for examining a couple or two partners.

Number 1

It is the partnership itself which creates the ability for the best work. It is advisable to watch out for selfishness. Egocentric behavior will harm the partnership.

The name of the game is joint work. The more the partners listen to each other, and the more consideration they show for one another's opinion, the more successful their joint endeavor will be. This is a constructive partnership. The resulting product might be a long-range one, leading to the creation of unique and path-breaking projects. This will only occur if there is a sense of togetherness and a suppression of the individual's desire to stand out.

Number 2

The partners have a productive relationship, though not an original one. They are excellent at accomplishing tasks, but are not inventive or innovative. Their connection is based on their ability to bring ideas to fruition and implement them in the best way possible. Number 2 indicates diligence and vigor.

Number 3

This indicates environmental action, the ability to be manipulative and a desire to be sophisticated. It is a good number for joint work. This number indicates that the partners are able to listen to and help their children (not necessarily only the couple's children, but rather the children of all participants in the group).

Number 4

This shows earthiness. The relationship between the partners will be good and significant, centering around joint creativity and new initiatives.

Number 5

This partnership will have an adventurous character. Number 5 predicts a great deal of action and endless energy. There is no time for rest. The need to keep going, move forward and meet the next challenge is the central and most important element.

Number 6

Family life is central to this relationship – a calm domestic scene. The partners will concentrate on bringing up their children and taking a lot of trouble with them (see Number 3). This number indicates patience, originality and creativity.

Number 7

This indicates groups and theories dealing with the occult and a connection with the unconscious.

Number 8

It is likely that there were many common factors in the past and they are manifesting themselves in the current incarnation. It is a good number for various endeavors related to money and property.

Number 9

The partners must be sensitive to the weaknesses of others, have a high degree of human sensitivity and be attentive to their inner voices. They must rely on their intuition and follow their hearts.

Numerology and the Upbringing of Children

How can numerology be applied to the upbringing of children? How can we direct parents to concentrate on those areas in which their child needs reinforcement?

There is a simple method: From the child's date of birth, take only the day of the month. Next, add just the last digit (the unit) of the year of birth and the sun sign (astrological sign) of the child (see below) – with Aries being 1 and Pisces being 12.

For example:

Birth date: 1.25.1995.

Astrological sign: Aquarius (11)

The day: 25

The year: 5

The sign: 11

2+5+5+1+1 = 14 = 1+4 = 5

In this case, 5 is the number which will direct the child's upbringing.

Numbers corresponding with the astrological signs:

Aries – 1; Taurus – 2; Gemini – 3; Cancer – 4; Leo – 5; Virgo – 6; Libra – 7; Scorpio – 8; Sagittarius – 9; Capricorn – 10;   Aquarius – 11;

Pisces – 12

Number 1

The general development of the child should be guided by freedom of choice. Encourage him in his attempts to experience new things. Reinforce his desire to include others and be an integrated, open individual. Help him develop his ability to be self-critical and to judge things objectively.

An approach which is too rigid will destroy his ability to be independent and make choices on his own. Give him freedom of choice and ample room to move, not limiting or stifling his actions. The more supportive his environment, the more balanced his fundamental characteristics will be.

If the child is given the opportunity to experience different things and face challenges on his own, he will develop self-confidence and will not be dependent on others. A child who is aware of danger will know how to take care of himself. His parents must remember that each child has to experiment on his own and learn to avoid mistakes through his own personal experience.

Even if he is aware of the failures of others, he will not always be careful until he has actually learned from his own experience. This is the way of the world, and parents must be aware of this and not force their opinions or authority on the child – an approach which might produce the opposite results.

Number 2

The Number 2 child is highly sensitive and needs a lot of help. He faces life with hesitation and imagines that it is full of danger. Life seems threatening and parents must do their best to give him a secure, solid base. He will find it easier to cope with the early years of life if he is in a warm familiar environment, surrounded by things he loves which are calming and make him happy.

The Number 2 child likes floating off into the world of the imagination. His imaginary experiences are so realistic to him that at times he loses himself in the stories he has made up. His parents must help him set boundaries between imagination and reality, and know when to put an end to his daydreaming and bring him back to earth. They are responsible for the child's mental well-being. Their child is very sensitive and they must be conscious of any change in his personality or any display of weakness or fear. Children do not explain themselves or their inner world very well. If the parents are not alert and do not identify problems in time to nip them in the bud, they run the risk of causing unintentional emotional damage which will later take a long time to repair.

Number 3

The Number 3 child is extraordinarily active. Parents must take a lot of trouble with him in order to ensure that he has outlets for his temperament.

If the parents are careful, they will be able to achieve several objectives at once: develop the child's imagination and thought processes, and enable him to release his inner energy via positive channels. The minute the parents let up, the child is liable to lose control completely. If active children are given due attention and taught to channel their energy in positive ways, they can become the type of adults who make a contribution to society, often assuming leadership roles in which they are heeded and followed by many people.

The Number 3 child needs a tremendous amount of warmth and love. He externalizes his emotions, and if he doesn't receive the attention he requires, he demands it in other ways.

He likes to use his imagination and play "make believe". He divides his world into clear categories of "good guys" and "bad guys". He is stubborn, and it is hard to get him to obey. Parents must learn to cope with his disobedience gently, and not in an authoritarian manner which will make him more aggressive and cause him to display violent behavior patterns.

Number 4

The Number 4 child requires stability. In times of need, he depends on the family unit and those closest to him for support. By providing him with warmth and love, the family serves as the most significant framework in his life. He is a "mama's boy". He likes to hide behind his mother's skirts and be as close to her as possible. His parents must try to give him a sense of stability which will help him deal with the difficulties he is bound to face in day-to-day life. The child must learn to adapt himself to the harsh surroundings in which we live. He must know that life is not always easy and that, at times, it is difficult to cope. He must learn to get along on his own. He must understand that Mom and Dad cannot be with him 24 hours a day, and that he will often have to make his own way in life. If he internalizes these principles and acquires a basic degree of confidence, he will be able to go out into the world and take upon himself tasks and decisions.

The Number 4 child is sensitive and full of compassion for every living being. He loves animals, and if it were up to him, the house would be full of abandoned creatures found in the street. He enjoys helping out and always volunteers for any task.

His highly developed imagination and sensitivity make him easily anxious and frightened. The parents must pay attention to his fears and help him overcome them. He should be encouraged to talk about his anxieties and express his fears concerning the outside world. Uncompromising support and an understanding of his difficulties are likely to help him to overcome these anxieties and fears.

Number 5

The Number 5 child's need for activity must be channeled in positive directions. He must be encouraged to get involved in sports. He has the ability to succeed in this area and it is therefore a good one to adopt. At the same time, he is also enchanted by stories and the arts. He can become totally engrossed in a riveting story. He has such a high level of concentration that he may detach himself completely from his surroundings. All branches of the arts interest him, but it is particularly worthwhile to focus on crafts such as carpentry, model-building (such as miniature airplanes), and other activities which require precision and patience. He needs to express himself and his talents, and is very active. He finds it easy to concentrate on a particular activity – but only if it fascinates him. If something interests him, he is able to keep at it for a lengthy period of time. If not, he will fritter the time away without any serious objective.

The child's concentration must be developed so that he will make the best use of his spare time. He requires both guidance and parents who are prepared to make an effort to give him the tools he needs. If he is not given a direction, he will go off the tracks. He does not have the ability to occupy himself and take an interest in something without external stimulation. It would be a shame if his talents were wasted and not properly exploited.

Number 6

The Number 6 child has a special sensitivity for beauty and harmony. He enjoys giving and receiving love, is sensitive to the beauty of the world and knows how to appreciate the loveliness of a flower or sense the joy of falling raindrops. He is excited by nature and knows how to express himself and involve others around him. His sensitivity to nature makes him an unusual child whose friends may not always understand what he is carrying on about. He is enthusiastic about things that other children tend to be indifferent to or take for granted. He is full of *joie de vivre*, and is temperamental and creative. He has artistic talents which he manifests by means of various projects, just like a little artist. He asks about anything he does not understand and wants to delve deeply into various phenomena and subjects. At times, it can prove tiring to his parents, who find it difficult to satisfy his curiosity. However, they should be pleased that he is inquisitive and knowledgeable, as this sets him apart from other children.

This type of child must be given a chance to express himself without being told what to do or how to think. His fertile imagination should be allowed to lead him and develop his ability for free and independent thought.

Number 7

The Number 7 child must learn to be open and attentive to others. He has a tendency to escape from reality into imaginary worlds. Relationships with others will force him to return to reality and face situations in which he will have to show determination and stand up for his rights. The parents' role is to provide him with the knowledge he will require to make his way through the complexities of life. He is able to give of himself limitlessly. He must be guided and made to understand the importance of setting limits in his relationships with others. He is not assertive. If he acquires the correct ways and behavior patterns, they will be useful to him throughout his life. His parents would do well to set him on a clear and correct path. Guidelines and directions – if given in the correct amount and at the appropriate time – will help him learn about the world he lives in. On the other hand, unnecessary interference, exaggerated demands and aggressive intrusion into his personal space will achieve the opposite results and undermine his self-confidence.

Number 8

This child is quite aggressive and requires restraint at an early age. If his parents do not pay due attention to the early stages of his development, the child might develop violent behavior patterns. Because of his active nature, he must constantly be in motion, and this is exhausting for the parents. However, they must not give up and allow the child too much freedom. They have to set limits and explain to him that we need order if we are to live in the world; he must take into account the limitations imposed by his environment. He knows how to express himself well and must therefore be encouraged to give vent to his tensions and aggressiveness in various ways. To do so, parents must be aware of the child's favorite means of expression. It might be in speech, the arts – such as music or painting – or sports. If the child is allowed to express himself freely and without coercion through one of these means, his aggressiveness and violent behavior are likely to decrease. This type of child needs a lot of warmth and love. Physical contact is important for sound emotional development for any child, and all the more so for this child.

If he learns to respect himself and his family, he will grow up knowing how to respect others and be sensitive to their feelings.

Number 9

Number 9 children take an interest in anything that comes their way. They are inquisitive. They are able to take things such as watches, etc. apart in order to see how they work. They are energetic, and, the same time, very sentimental. They must be supported during times of pressure and not be expected to cope on their own, particularly during the first stages of life. Emotional support is likely to strengthen them considerably.

They are aware of the plight of others, and are interested in and fascinated by the pain in the world. Their sense of social justice is highly developed, and even at a tender age they know how to give to others. They inquire about the reasons for life's injustices and problems.

These children will grow up to be concerned citizens. If their sensitivity towards others is brought to the fore and not suppressed by the environment, both they and society will benefit when they mature.

Your "Sexual Number"

Sexuality is an important area of numerology. For this purpose, we utilize the personal number, or just the number resulting from the first name, or the number resulting from one's nickname – according to the professional or amateur numerologist's choice.

The interpretation emphasizes sexuality, taking into account the relationship of the partners.

Number 1

These people conduct their sex lives in a serious manner. Their general behavior is rational, and this is also reflected in their sexual relationships. They are able to orchestrate a sexual encounter through manipulative and sophisticated means.

Expressing emotions is not their strong point. To the casual observer, it seems that they are cold, without emotion. However, this is not true. They are able to express warm, heart-felt feelings – but only if they really love someone. Then they are willing to give of themselves boundlessly.

Number 2

Number 2 people like variety in their sex life. They quickly tire of a steady partner if he/she does not provide constant stimulation and innovation. They enjoy changing partners frequently. Even more than the pleasure derived from the relationship and the actual love-making, they enjoy the preceding ritual. It is the effort they make to attract their partner as well as the conquest itself that gives them great satisfaction. Soon after the initial sexual excitement disappears, they get tired of their partner and are ready to move on to their next conquest.

Number 3

Sex is central to Number 3's relationships. It results from an honest expression of the emotions of affection and love. Number 3's partners may be sure that he/she loves them whole-heartedly. These people do not betray their partners or allow their eye to rove. They are satisfied with their lovers and invest all their efforts and sexual energies in them.

They enjoy any form or technique of sex and indulge in it as often as possible. They like varying their sex life and altering the location, place or position.

Number 4

These people find it difficult to start new relationships. However, when they do make the effort to build a new relationship, it is long-lasting.

They are passionate lovers and sex is important to them, though not the major component in their relationship with their partner. They enjoy making love so much that at times it seems that they wait impatiently for the end of the work day simply to jump into bed with their partner. They are sensual – each of the senses is involved in love-making. They like to spoil their partners, and to stroke, feel, smell and taste their partner's body.

Number 5

Number 5 people always feel that they are missing out on something better – even when in a relationship with a partner. When they do not have a steady partner, they sleep around. They behave as if they do not have enough time left and must take large, hurried bites out of the fruit of passion before it disappears. They leave behind them a string of disappointed and humiliated partners, who feel that they have been exploited. Directly following love-making, they are capable of thinking of the next target they intend to pursue.

If they are happily married, it is thanks to their partner's numbers which are the moderating factor, permitting a relationship with Number 5.

Number 6

Love is honest and feelings are deep when it comes to Number 6. They are not able to make love with someone without a firm basis for an emotional connection. They are very sentimental and romantic. They enjoy having sex by candlelight and with soft music playing in the background. They are the perfect lovers. They will always surprise their partner with a bottle of wine, a bouquet of flowers or a small gift. More than the need to make love, they need the expressions of affection that accompany love-making –

hugs, kisses and foreplay. They are able to spend long hours giving physical attention to their partners in the form of massage, endless stroking, etc. As spouses, they are also warm, continuing to maintain a relationship of generous giving to their partners.

Number 7

Number 7 people, being shy, do not have sex with a partner unless they are convinced of their partner's full-hearted love. They will not be open or free during sex unless they are sure of their partner's love, and know that he will accept them as they are – without any danger of being hurt by tactless words. When they give of themselves to their partner, they do so with all their heart.

They usually enter into a relationship whole-heartedly, in a manner which ensures that it will be especially long-lasting.

Number 8

Number 8 people enjoy sex very much and for them it is the spice of life. However, they are very calculating and do not form casual relationships. They think and plan ahead and tend to have serious relationships. Sex is so important to them that even if they met their knight in shining armor – the perfect partner – they would not be able to have a serious relationship with him unless the sexual aspect was flawless. Sex stands above everything else.

Number 9

These people like to have sexual relationships with one partner, over a long period of time, knowing that he or she is theirs. Just as they do not betray their spouses, they expect their partners to be faithful to them. They are not warm family people.

Challenges

Challenges are the special tasks a person has to face in his life. The most effective method for arriving at a person's Challenge Number – in other words, to know the single most important thing that he must deal with now – is to calculate the difference between the last name and the first name.

For example:

SARAH PETERS

SARAH: 1+1+9+1+8 = 20 = 2

PETERS: 7+5+2+5+9+1 = 29 = 7

The difference between 7 and 2 is 5, and that is the challenge number.

Pay attention to three important principles:

1. Only the difference is taken into consideration and not its value (positive or negative).

2. Number 9 is not considered a challenge number. When both the first name and the last name are 9, the challenge number will be 3.

3. If the numbers of the first and last names are identical (except for Number 9), that number is the challenge number.

Number 1

Something is keeping you from progressing along your path to fulfillment. Do not let crises that may occur cause you to lose your determination. If you have emotional problems that are liable to slow you down or lead to a loss of control, do not give up. It is worthwhile to have them seen to in order to increase your ability and inner capacity to cope with inevitable conflict.

If you wish to develop and not surrender to trends dictated by the period you live in, listen to your inner voice and convince yourself that you *are* able to overcome the little ups and downs of life. These are just "background noise" and will disappear in time. Do not attribute too much significance to them, otherwise you might give up and feel helpless.

Others are just as important as you are. Even if it seems that somebody else's world is very different than ours, and that his or her behavioral codes are unfamiliar and foreign to us, remember that we have all been cut from the same cloth.

With a little good will and openness, you may arrive at the desired understanding and harmony. The more we understand and learn to accept people's complexity and the differences between them, the more we will understand the world. Adapting ourselves to our surroundings is important and will affect the course of our lives.

Number 2

You are too spiritual. You should be aware of the boundary between normal sensitivity and turning this sensitivity into a catalyst for fears and anxiety. Awareness of these feelings is very important, as it is liable to have a very significant influence on the future. If jealousy is too strong, it is likely to lead to self-hatred.

The ability to forgive is one of the central elements on the road to wholeness. It is dependent on one's general abilities and particularly upon the relationships one develops with others. Truth will emerge in the end, and the preservation of spiritual unity should be one of the most important tasks in life.

Be aware of your desires and abilities, set the rules for yourself, and decide what the appropriate direction for yourself is. The more control you exert – over your personality, your needs, desires and aspirations – the more power and inner strength you will acquire.

Number 3

You have not realized your potential. You do not let yourself go "all the way" with your ideas. Something is blocking your path to full freedom. You have a mental block which prevents you from attaining emotional and mental liberation.

It may result from unconscious fears. Try to free yourself from these emotional and mental confines and let the art in you burst out in its full glory. The more freedom you allow your feelings, the easier it will be for your artistic expression to reach the inner truth which is bottled up inside you and until now has not been able to escape.

Set objectives for yourself and try to attain them. It is important for you to be involved in only a few areas, getting the most out of them, rather than spreading yourself too thinly and not having the chance to explore each field and derive the maximum from it.

Do not take a defensive position vis-a-vis the external world. The more you become open to criticism, flexible in your thought processes and receptive to new ideas, the closer you will come to achieving two objectives: a finished product of better quality, and friends who appreciate your ability to cooperate and evolve.

You must be careful and aware.

Number 4

This person sees the trees, but not the forest! Perfectionism is now more dominant than ever. You consider it very important to be precise at your work, and do not like sloppy or unfinished endeavors. Make sure you preserve your self-discipline. It helps you to be an organized and responsible person. You dislike disorder – a quality which is quite apparent in your personality. This is not the time for spontaneity or activities which require physical exertion. If you want to achieve good results, it is crucial that you concentrate on the work at hand.

You are too caught up in trivial subtleties which slow you down and make you seem petty. This is not the quickest or most convenient way to attain your goals.

Details may be important, but do not get carried away.

Learn to control your impulses and urges. This is not difficult for you, thanks to your orderly and disciplined nature. Do not be tempted to get involved in insignificant activities. Preserve the solid principles you have always upheld. It is possible that you will be obliged to cope with delays. However, they are most probably not the result of anything you did. Take care that the things that *do* depend on you are being done in the orderly and efficiently manner you like.

Number 5

Impulse dominates, not logic! Inside you, things are stormy and you seek ways of releasing tensions. However, reality dictates a daily routine which suppresses your boiling passions. Although it seems almost impossible, if you were to consider the significance and purpose of your daily tasks, you might be able to moderate your desires more easily.

You do not have the patience to wait for the right timing, the right moment. Your energy – threatening to explode outwards and release tension – could be directed to positive channels, such as business trips.

If you suppress your impulses and do not allow yourself to give vent to them, you may become frustrated or depressed. Do not let yourself get into that situation. Learn to direct your energies into positive channels immediately and use them for doing useful things, both for yourself and for society. The feedback you receive from the environment is likely to be an appropriate compensation for your efforts. Positive feedback will help charge your positive energies.

Number 6

You are tied to others – at times, too much so. You enjoy giving warmth and giving of yourself to others. The more another person benefits from your attention, and the more you view yourself as being able to fulfill another person's wishes and expectations, the happier you are.

You have a tendency to bend the rules and not follow them to the letter. You enjoy making the rules yourself and find it difficult to operate under conditions in which someone else has laid down the law. You find it hard to accept that others might have similar abilities to yours and might know more than you do. You have to accept the fact that there are people who are no less talented than you are.

Learn to control your inherent tendency to generalize. Be aware of the fact that even entire groups are composed of individuals and that each one is a world unto himself. The more you get to know people from various backgrounds, ethnic groups, nations, and so on, the easier it will be for you to stop generalizing. Keep an open mind. It might change your world-view in the future.

Number 7

You tend to escape from reality. You are not master of your needs. You let yourself be swept away by your urges and cannot control them. You are led by your beliefs and not by rational thought, which has lost its grip on your life. You have lost your power of judgment regarding yourself, and, obviously, regarding your environment. You have lost your self-respect and abilities. You are constantly fearful, making it difficulty for you to live day-to-day life. Your social life is dull and you cannot find a cure for your malaise.

Spiritual reform is required. You should examine how you relate to life and to the society in which you live. Replacing the present environment with one in which you will develop a sense of caring for your surroundings, friends and family, will invigorate you and give you a new lease of life which is worth working toward.

Number 8

You only see one side of things – either the material or the spiritual! In both cases, it is important not to be too extreme. Take the middle road, not only as concerns these two central factors in life – the material and the spiritual – but also regarding the practical aspects of life, conceptual understanding of ideas, as well as education and teaching. Moderation and compromise are likely to bridge gaps and lead to a harmonious life. On the other hand, an extreme world-view will cause a deterioration in your relationships with others, a polarization, and an inability to bridge gaps in your life.

Number 9

This is not a challenge number.

The Number of Spiritual Calling

This number indicates the spiritual, mystical, magical calling of our existence. We reach it by choosing the first and last letters of the first and last names.

For example:
SARA**H** **P**ETER**S**
1+8+7+1 = 17 = 8

Checking the interpretation for Number 8, we will understand what our calling in life is and how it guides us.

Number 1

This number indicates initiative and primality. It is advisable to develop these qualities, which are positive qualities that characterize you. It is important to develop the ability not to depend on others, but to concentrate on the "self" and know how to suffer consequences, even if your mistakes are unexpectedly big. Never place the blame on others. Know how to defend your rights, and avoid groveling or being spineless. At times, taking a tough position is necessary. However, it is crucial that your ability to be a leader not be accompanied by negative qualities such as bossiness and aggressiveness. Self-control is important. You will only reach positive results if you subdue your personal desires by means of your abilities and talents.

Number 2

This number indicates sensitivity to and consideration for others, an aspiration to mental tranquillity and calmness, as well as the search for equilibrium. Personal development is also likely to be facilitated by adopting feminine or maternal qualities: caring, the desire to protect the small and weak, and a longing for wholeness.

Number 3

It is advisable to develop special talents and skills and your ability to express your "self" in the most original way possible. The ability to communicate and express yourself is very important. If you have difficulties communicating, you should learn how to overcome them, thereby releasing tensions, solving problems resulting from this lack of communication or flawed communication, sharpening your communicative skills and learning how to listen.

If until now you have seen the glass as half-empty and tended to be pessimistic, it is now time to adopt a more positive approach, trying to see the full half and the positive sides of various situations. A positive approach will bring light and *joie de vivre* into your life. The search for joy is not a casual one. Happiness and *joie de vivre* are the highest goals that we strive to reach throughout our lives.

Number 4

It is crucial that you control your urges and impulses. The less control you exercise, the more animal-like you will become. Restraining your impulses is the most important thing for you, as well as learning to delay gratification. The desire to obtain everything quickly, here and now, which is characteristic of our times, works against us. Learn to be practical, setting goals and trying to reach them using appropriate means and without taking any shortcuts. It is important to be as efficient as possible. Practicality and efficiency will help you to attain your goals in the optimal way.

You must develop a realistic view of life and not get caught up in dreams and ideas that lead nowhere. The less "dreamy" you are and the more your feet are planted firmly on the ground, the easier it will be to develop your ideas and bring them to fruition.

Number 5

You must strive to understand others. Harness your intuitive ability and develop a sensitivity to the needs of society and the general good. It is crucial that you learn to open up and adapt more easily to new situations. If you do so, you will meet new people and broaden your horizons in various fields. Know the boundaries between genuine interest in someone else's life and inquisitiveness. It is important to keep your curiosity in check. Do not be impulsive. Do not neglect unfinished endeavors and move on to new things before completing the old. Inexplicable outbursts may be detrimental to you. Think twice before having an angry outburst. There is no doubt that there are other ways to express rage or distress, without causing those around you to recoil.

Number 6

Seek love! If you give of yourself boundlessly, you will find that love is returned in the same measure, but through different means. If you have unique abilities allowing you to serve and be helpful to others, you might accomplish this in the emotional, and not just the physical realm. You have good analytical tools which enable you to offer practical and constructive advice to others and to solve many of their problems in various areas of life.

Your commendable approach to the arts opens up new channels that you were not aware of until now. Sculpture, painting, music or dance may serve as constructive and empowering activities.

Number 7

This is a number which indicates the nature of the spiritual stuff we are made of and the development of spirituality through mysticism. The search itself and the process of trial and error are important. Do not cease wondering, investigating and examining the essence of things. Develop self-confidence – it is important and fundamental. Focus on it and use it as a starting-point for your spiritual journeys. Only after you have become familiar with your "self" and its essence will you be able to return to yourself following each journey which separates you from the solid ground of reality. Meditation may be a wonderful way in which to explore your soul and personal development. It is worth your while to utilize it as an additional tool on your path to help you know your place in the universe.

Number 8

This indicates honesty, purity of heart and patience. These are the basic qualities for communication with other people. Do not give in, even if you have to work hard to reach these lofty qualities. Develop a sense of justice and be aware of all the subtleties when it comes to situations of injustice. You have leadership qualities and the ability to get others to follow you. Be aware of values, as they form the basis of the world; sensitivity to these values is important in understanding the ways in which the world functions.

Number 9

Develop your abilities in the realm of the spirit. Do not forfeit your privilege to be a leader. Your special talents allow you to see the unseen and explore spiritual worlds. Listen to your inner voice and pay attention to inner directives, which show you the right and true path. You should be as creative as possible in order to release tension and relieve physical and mental stress. Work toward improving humanity, contribute to the greater good and be attentive to society's needs, not only to your own. It is important to make an effort to help others and take advantage of your abilities and skills in order to attain higher objectives. Do not focus just on yourself. Your contribution to humanity can be significant only if you learn to be consistent in your efforts to achieve the goals you set yourself. Draw upon your patience and staying power.

The Number of Influence

The number of influence indicates the factor or factors that determine the shape of a person's path in life. This number results from the sum of the person's first name number and his/her mother's name number.

For example: **SARAH** daughter of **RACHEL**
SARAH: 1+1+9+1+8 = 20
RACHEL: 9+1+3+8+5+3 = 29
SARAH + RACHEL = 49 = 4+9 = 13 = 1+3 = 4
The number of influence is therefore 4.

This number *does not* change if one's first name is changed. The name which determines the number of influence is the name one receives at birth.

Number 1
Number 1 people always prefer to rely on themselves and their personal experience. They will never learn from the experience of others, even if they are convinced of its correctness and veracity. Even if they *do* ask advice of others, they do not apply it.

This behavior leads to the extreme egocentricity with which they relate to their surroundings. They must moderate their feelings of superiority and concentrate more on others and less on themselves. In the end, they will benefit, as they will be given more sympathy and affection. This might help them and soften them up. Their lives will be less rigid and more pleasant.

Even though they are hard on themselves and on those around them, they are their own masters, and their accomplishments are theirs alone. They do not share success, since they always work alone. They are usually quite inventive. They are self-motivated, neither depending on others nor delegating responsibilities.

Number 1 people are very active. They enjoy being in constant motion and are always busy, never tiring. The results they achieve are considerable. Their achievements, which are significant, exert a great influence on their surroundings.

Number 2

The key word for Number 2 people is "together". They get their best results when collaborating with others. They enjoy working in teams or pairs; their results would not be as good if they were to work alone. To succeed in life, they need to be surrounded by people with whom they can create things, and from whom they receive feedback and comments.

They are usually very laid-back and easy to get along with. They are not stubborn and tend to give in easily. They will do anything to prevent a quarrel and to smooth over possible differences of opinion.

These people have no problem sharing with others, even when it come to the things that are most valuable to them. They enjoy pleasing others and it is very important to them to be liked. They are vulnerable, and seemingly insignificant things are liable to hurt them very deeply. At the same time, they tend to forgive easily and do not bear grudges.

On the emotional level, they are extremely sensitive. On occasion, this quality is perceived as a weakness by others, who are easily tempted to take advantage of Number 2 people for their own personal benefit. Number 2s must be aware of this and find the fine line between doing favors for others and being taken advantage of by them thoughtlessly.

Number 3

These people are not very patient by nature. They like to see quick results – here and now! Aggressiveness is one of their dominant characteristics. If they take on a challenge, they do not give up easily, even if they are not completely sure that it is feasible.

They have a high level of self-awareness and are conscious of their special abilities; they are therefore almost always successful. At the same time, others tend to shy away from them.

Their combination of arrogance, self-importance and success does not endear them to most people. They are winners and calculate their actions wisely. They set clear goals and usually find it easy to attain them. They will not hesitate to employ unorthodox means to achieve their objectives.

They are manipulative and sly. They know how to fit in everywhere, and immediately grasp the rules of the game. They have a highly developed ability to adapt to new situations and are thick-skinned. They are not easily hurt and tend to ignore hints that they are not welcome in a particular place.

They can be extremely generous, although it usually transpires that their motives for this are distinctly selfish. On the other hand, they are warm family people, concerned with their loved ones' welfare and jealously guarding it.

Number 4

Number 4 people know exactly what direction they are going in and have little difficulty overcoming the obstacles on their path. They have the ability to think logically, not emotionally. They stick to the facts and are able to judge situations according to the principles of justice, without sentimentality. They are pompous. They do not need many friends. However, they appreciate and cherish the few close friends they have.

They are in favor of hard work and are willing to expend much time and effort in the pursuit of good results. Money and financial success are central to them, but do not constitute a goal in themselves. Number 4s are law-abiding in the extreme and have solid, uncompromising ideals. They enjoy spending their leisure time at home within the family unit. They prefer being at home to going out to cafés or clubs, and keep away from large parties or festivities. They adore books, newspapers and journals. They have highly developed verbal skills and express themselves well in writing, too. They enjoy dabbling in writing from time to time, but the fruits of their labors usually remain in the drawer, unpublished. This is due to two main factors: first, the fact that they are perfectionists and are not sure that their creation is perfect, and second, because they fear criticism. They find it difficult to accept criticism in view of their high opinion of themselves. If they learned to be more involved in society and to appreciate others, they wouldl profit by it.

Number 5

Number 5 people radiate a great deal of personal charm. It stands them in good stead when they find themselves in tricky situations, which they tend to fall into very easily. They are constantly active, never take a moment to rest, and run around endlessly. They not only exhaust themselves – they wear out those around them, who suffer from all this excess energy. Number 5s would be well advised to learn to control their desire for so much activity.

These people are impulsive and complain constantly – generally without justification. They would do well to slow down their pace and put things into their correct perspective. This would save them a lot of unnecessary distress.

Their strength lies in their extraordinary ability to adapt to their surroundings. They are superbly articulate and are good communicators. They are liked by friends and by those they encounter in their daily dealings. Their ability to spread love, warmth and affection around them is great. Therefore, people find it easy to love them back – and they certainly need large amounts of love. They know how to behave in order to attract others. They are excellent at intimate relationships with a partner – both in sex and in love and romance.

Number 5 people are sentimental and know that they may expose their hearts without the fear that it makes them appear too weak or soft. Loving others is the most central thing in their lives, and they spare nothing in the attempt to enrich their emotional and marital lives.

Number 6

These are highly spiritual people who are attracted to the arts. Their purpose in life is to help others. They feel that the essence of happiness is to serve humanity, and they always have a positive attitude toward life. They see the bright side of any negative situation and emphasize it. They are accompanied by optimism throughout their lives. They draw their strength from their honest, real feelings and from the love they receive from those around them – love which they reciprocate. They do not hesitate to give of themselves to society and believe that one should "cast his bread upon the water."

They are creative and original people who know how to extricate themselves from uncomfortable situations and improvise if necessary.

They pursue neither wealth nor financial security. They make do with love alone and nurture their inner happiness. It is important to them to spread the message of "Love thy neighbor." They aspire to peace and human freedom. In their view, this is their basic purpose on earth.

They are generally responsible, but at times may err out of naiveté or due to an innocent belief in the honest intentions of others. They are stable, yet enjoy drifting in other worlds. One can easily catch them "spaced out" or day-dreaming. They should stay in touch with reality and be more realistic when it comes to human nature.

Number 7

These people do not assume anything! They always try to get to the bottom of an issue, investigating it and getting as much out of it as possible. They have very defined opinions and are not willing to lower their standards or compromise their principles in order to be one of the gang or to win favor.

Many have white collar jobs. Usually, they are found behind a desk, busy with paperwork or writing which demands profound thought or extensive discussion.

Number 7 people have a direction in life that is based on education. This is the key to their success. They are concerned with the quality of life and the world we live in, and try to do everything in their power to make a contribution to these causes. Occasionally, they become so excited and obsessed with some idea that they overwhelm those around them and are even liable to cause themselves to be ostracized. They must be aware of this and try to avoid adopting extreme standpoints.

Number 7 people are spiritual. However, besides their natural desire to improve the world, they do not have far-reaching ambitions. They settle for little and lead calm, quiet lives. They do not get into unnecessary arguments and always try to smooth over any disagreements or differences of opinion that may arise. They are laid-back and calm, easy to get along with and pleasant to live with. They are interesting and wise conversationalists, and there is always something to learn from them.

Number 8

These people are controlled by their strong desire for wealth and economic power. They love the good life. They are hedonists who know how to utilize the material for the benefit of the spirit. Their objectives are very clear. They believe that, with the exception of health, anything can be obtained by means of money. This is their guiding-light. They aspire to positions of status and economic power with the sole aim of providing themselves with a better and more pleasant lifestyle.

They are not ostentatious and keep their private pleasures to themselves. While they are not modest to the point of concealing their wealth, neither do they flaunt it in public or boast of their accomplishments. It is enough for them to know that they can enjoy their wealth. They do not like to save. They are big spenders and like to give generously. At the same time, they are very possessive of their work place or business, and are liable to become extremely belligerent if their status is threatened.

These are assertive people who are aware of their power. They are honest and will never get anything by deception or unorthodox means. Those who meet them tend to like them because of their good qualities. People are not envious of them, because they are open and desire to give to others and improve their surroundings. Whenever the need to help arises, they will be the first – and always generously.

They are not particularly warm family people, but are always concerned with their family's needs and are available when needed. Business is their highest priority, but in the end, it may be said that they are conscious of the power of the family and its ability to serve as a catalyst and motivating force behind a good business and a happy life.

Number 9

The positive energies they receive from the love of those around them motivate Number 9s to work on behalf of humanity. Without this love they would be lost – like a flower with no water. This is their driving force in life.

They are very sensitive to others and their weaknesses and would never hurt a fly. They do not have the tendency to torment, bother or embarrass others. Because of their desire to avoid embarrassing situations, they suppress certain energies and tensions which are then released in other ways, such as in the form of incomprehensible and inexplicable outbursts.

When they know what they are working toward and what they are aspiring to, they are very determined to succeed. At times, they are liable to fail and be disappointed time and time again. However, they possess great inner strength. They do not give up, and return to the battle once again.

These people are responsible and dependable; they never disappoint the people who turn to them for help. They always find the right words to say and know how to cheer people up and boost morale. Thanks to their responsible nature, they are careful not to give bad advice or delude others. They have a lot of power and the ability to exert a great influence on their environment. They do not abuse this trait and always work toward helping others.